ANDREA DORIA AND OTHER RECENT LINER DISASTERS

William H. Miller

AMBERLEY

First published 2016

Amberley Publishing
The Hill, Stroud
Gloucestershire, GL5 4EP

www.amberley-books.com

Copyright © William H. Miller, 2016

The right of William H. Miller to be identified
as the Author of this work has been asserted in
accordance with the Copyrights, Designs and
Patents Act 1988.

ISBN 978 1 4456 6129 2 (print)
ISBN 978 1 4456 6130 8 (ebook)

British Library Cataloguing in Publication Data.
A catalogue record for this book is available from
the British Library.

Typeset in 10pt on 13pt Celeste.
Typesetting by Amberley Publishing.
Printed in the UK.

Contents

Foreword by John Moyer

The first time I remember hearing about the *Andrea Doria* was in 1975 at a shipwreck artifact show in Brielle, NJ, put on by the Eastern Divers Association. I was in the middle of taking my Basic Scuba course and my instructor took me to meet some of his friends. I met some divers who told me about a wreck they described as the 'Mount Everest of Diving'. It was a massive 700-foot-long passenger liner lying on its starboard side, 240 feet deep in the cold, dark waters of the North Atlantic. That area of the ocean is known for frequent storms, rough seas and strong currents. They said you often have to pull yourself hand over hand down the anchor line, fighting to reach the bottom. Visibility averages about 25 feet, so they had to be careful not to get hung up in the commercial fishing nets that had snagged on the exterior of the wreck over the years. Because it's on its side, it's easy to become disoriented when penetrating the wreck. The interior is a confusing maze of ceilings and floors that are now walls, walls that are now ceilings and floors, and stairwells that run sideways. It is filled with silt, so the water may be clear when you swim into the wreck but, as soon as you pick something up, you're engulfed in a cloud and visibility goes to zero. Sometimes you have to memorize your route and feel your way out of the wreck. There are also many steel cables and wires hanging down that are easy to get tangled in. They explained to me that the wreck is located in the middle of the shipping lanes of the approaches to New York harbor, so there is always a risk of getting run over by a tanker or freighter while anchored in the wreck. When I left the show, I knew I wanted to see the *Andrea Doria* for myself.

My first dives on the wreck were in 1982 with a small group of divers who had chartered a boat to take us out to the wreck for three days. We anchored into the forward end of the promenade deck and I made four dives exploring the area. My very first finds were two silver jewelry boxes and a brass-framed window. The next year we began diving into the ship's first-class dining room where we found piles of china, glassware, silverware and cups and saucers. In 1985, I was part of the team that spent a week on the wreck and recovered the 200-lb brass bell from the ship's after steering station.

After the 1985 trip I began my serious research on the ship and collected everything I could find related to the *Andrea Doria*. I traveled to Italy to meet with the engineers at Ansaldo Shipyards, who had designed the ship, and Italia Line senior officers who had served on the *Andrea Doria* since she was launched and were onboard the night of the collision. I also interviewed as many passengers as I could find to hear about their experiences. In the years from 1985 to 1992 we made many trips out to the site, exploring new areas of the wreck and recovering whatever artifacts we found.

In 1993, I chartered the research vessel *Wahoo* and assembled twelve of the most experienced deep-wreck divers in the US and Canada. Our mission was to recover two 1000-lb ceramic sculptures from deep inside the wreck. They were created by one of Italy's greatest ceramic artists, Guido Gambone, and displayed in the ship's Winter Garden Lounge. We discovered that they had fallen from their mounts and were lying on the interior wall [now the floor]. Over a period of four days, working at a depth of 200 feet in near zero visibility, each one was rigged with inflatable lift bags and floated to the surface.

Prior to the expedition, we had filed legal papers in the US District Court in Camden, NJ. Judge Joseph Rodriguez granted an Admiralty Arrest, asserting the court's jurisdiction over the *Doria* and appointed me custodian of the wreck. This required attaching a sealed canister containing the arrest papers to the wreck. Later in the year I again appeared before Judge Rodriquez. My attorney argued that, although insured by an Italian consortium, the underwriters had made no attempt at salvage in nearly forty years. Therefore, they had abandoned the wreck. The court agreed and granted me exclusive salvage rights, clear title, and ownership to any artifacts recovered. Each year we are required to submit a report to the court detailing our dives and our plans for the next dive season. In his ruling, the judge stated: 'Moyer's independent research and archeological documentation of his salvage efforts indicate a respect for the *Andrea Doria* as something more than just a commercial salvage project.'

The decay of sunken ships is slow and most often unobserved. The sinking of the *Andrea Doria* produced a wreck of very unusual characteristics. Due to the newsreel camera planes circling overhead, it became world famous and it is in water that is accessible to divers. As a result, the wreck has been continually visited by amateur and commercial divers since its sinking sixty years ago. Peter Gimbel was the first diver on the wreck just 28 hours after it sank. Other than the huge collision hole on the starboard side, he saw no obvious damage to the ship. Since then divers have been reporting major decay events on the wreck. The wheelhouse was still intact when Italian divers filmed it in 1968, but gone by 1973. The top three decks of the superstructure had fallen off by the time I first dove it in 1982. We used the port-side bridge wing as a landmark until it fell off in the early 1990s. The Winter Garden was completely intact when we recovered the Gambone sculptures in 1993, but collapsed only two years later. Later in the 1990s, we noted cracks in the hull, while the boat deck, upper deck, and foyer deck had started to slide downward to the sea floor. Recently the cracks have expanded and the hull has entered its final stage of a flattening process that will someday result in an unrecognizable pile of debris on the bottom of the sea.

Fortunately, we have been able to rescue many historically important artifacts and unique works of art before they were lost forever.

John Moyer

Foreword by Marianne Florio

My grandparents came to America as immigrants, landing at Ellis Island and later settling near Hartford. Typically, they worked hard, very hard in fact. My grandmother was an excellent cook and my grandfather had good business skills. By the 1950s, they owned three restaurants, each Italian of course, and were proud of their success in America. In 1956, they decided to take my parents, my brother, sister and myself to Italy to see relatives. It was my grandparents' first return to their homeland in over forty years. Times there had changed and there were relatives to see – and, of course, to tell about their American success. All of us went down to New York, to Pier 84 as I remember, to board the *Cristoforo Colombo* for the crossing to Naples. It was so exciting! A big ocean liner, crossing the ocean, summer fun. To me, it was like something from a movie, one of those romantic Hollywood movies. My brother, sister and I had our own cabin. We were in cabin class, which was, we were told, less stuffy and less formal than first class. There were other families aboard as well and so we made shipboard friends. The weather was warm, and we enjoyed the ship's outdoor pool each and every day. There were also special events such as kids' games and an ice cream party in the afternoon. For my grandparents and parents, they had nighttime dancing, horse racing (with wooden horses) and ship's bingo, which my grandmother never missed. I remember the food, often very Italian and which my grandmother praised. I also remember having a crush on our waiter. His name was Paolo and, to me, he looked like a movie star. He might have been thirty, but seemed so mature, so sophisticated. I could barely speak when he came to the table. There were also, as I remember, midnight buffets with everything and anything you could imagine, set around these great ice carvings. I especially remember a huge swordfish made of ice.

We stayed in Italy for three weeks. We were booked to return to New York in early August, but on the *Cristoforo Colombo's* sister ship, the *Andrea Doria*. My grandparents wanted to return before the summer's end, before Labor Day. We began to count the days until the sailing from Naples. Then, suddenly, we heard the news: the *Andrea Doria* would not be returning to Italy. We would not be sailing. After a collision, it sank on July 26th. All of Italy seemed to be in mourning, deep mourning. One of the country's newest and most beautiful ocean liners was gone. It was a national tragedy. But how and when would we return?

My father later took charge and contacted the Italian Line office. After some uncertainty and shuffling, we would sail in mid-August but on the *Conte Biancamano*. She was an older ship, not quite as luxurious or as beautiful as the *Andrea Doria*. We were called '*Andrea Doria* extras', passengers who needed alternate passage to New York. I recall there were about fifty Catholic priests and nuns aboard. They had been to the Vatican and blessed by Pope Pius XII. During that return trip, I recall little talk of the *Andrea Doria* and the sinking. It was like some dead relative – no one wanted to mention it, it was too sad. But I do remember the nuns praying. One of them told me that they were specially praying to God for a safe voyage to New York.

I attended Bill's wonderful, nostalgia-filled talks about the great liners and, while we were sailing from England to New York aboard the *Queen Mary 2* in May 2015, he mentioned his work on a future book about the *Andrea Doria* and other ocean liner diasters. I am both delighted and honored to contribute this foreword, my ocean travel memories from the 1950s.

Marianne Florio

Acknowledgements

With the rescue or salvage of a troubled ship, it takes many hands to see the process through. It is much the same with a book – many hands take part. First and foremost, my best thanks to Amberley Publications and Connor Stait and his team for taking this title on and seeing it through. Special appreciation also to John Moyer and Marianne Florio for their reflective forewords, and to Moss Hill for his long and detailed recollections of the sinking of the *Oceanos* and *Achille Lauro*. And to Michael Hadgis for his technical expertise and support.

Additional 'hands onboard', and who have my great thanks as well, include Ernest Arroyo, the late Frank Braynard, Captain Helge Brudvik, Michael Cassar, Tom Cassidy, Anthony Cook, Luis Miguel Correia, the late Frank Cronican, Maurizio Eliseo, Richard Faber, Hans Hoffmann, David Hutchings, Des Kirkpatrick, Norman Knebel, Peter Knego, Anthony La Forgia, the late Abe Michaelson, Dr James Merrill, Fred Rodriguez, Sal Scannella, Captain Klaus Schacht, the late Antonio Scrimali, the late Der Scutt, Roger Sherlock, Captain Ed Squire, Stephen L. Tacey, Michael Tsaler, Everett Viez, Richard Weiss and Al Wilhelmi.

Companies and organizations that have assisted include: British India Steam Navigation Company, Costa Cruises, Crystal Cruises, Cunard Line, Flying Camera Inc, Hoboken Historical Museum, Moran Towing & Transportation Co, Port Authority of New York & New Jersey, Royal Mail Lines, South African Air Force, South Street Seaport Museum, Steamship Historical Society of America, Time-Life Inc, United States Coast Guard, World Ocean & Cruise Liner Society and World Ship Society.

My humble apologies to anyone overlooked.

Introduction

The sinking of the *Andrea Doria* remains one of the most famous maritime disasters of the twentieth century. Myself, I well remember the television newscasts and newspaper headlines on the morning of 26 July 1956. The *Doria* had been rammed the night before by another liner, Sweden's *Stockholm*. It all seemed too sad, tragic, almost incomprehensible. I was in disbelief. How could the *Andrea Doria* sink? Perhaps it was all a mistake. Still a schoolboy, but already a devoted follower and observer of the great liners, I was puzzled. I asked a special favor of my father: would he take me by car a day later, the 27th, from Hoboken to the cliffs of nearby Weehawken to make absolutely sure that the *Andrea Doria* had not arrived. She was due at Pier 84, at the foot of West 44th Street in midtown Manhattan and just across from Weehawken, on the morning of the 26th. Soon after we arrived, I looked across, in the fading light of a summer's evening, and the berth at Pier 84 was indeed empty. The *Andrea Doria* had not arrived as scheduled. Yes, she had sunk – the news reports were correct. Some thirteen New York City blocks north, the smallish, all-white *Stockholm* was in port. She had returned after having made an 11.30 a.m. departure two days before, on Wednesday the 25th. She was again at Swedish American Line's terminal, Pier 97 at the foot of West 57th Street. She had not been due back in New York harbor for another month, in late August. The *Stockholm* was never one of the big, more imposing Atlantic liners – she was actually more of a passenger-cargo ship. But she seemed especially small on that July evening. Like a bad child, she almost seemed to be hiding, in disgrace, fearing punishment. To most, she was already the villain, the less important little ship that sank the very important flagship of the entire Italian merchant marine and one of the post-Second World War era's finest new ocean liners.

The late Frank Braynard was one of the world's greatest maritime historians, authors and artists. He was also my dear friend, mentor and role model. He later told me that, near midnight on the night of the 25th, he received a phone call from CBS Radio. Frank was at home, some forty miles east of midtown Manhattan, in Sea Cliff on Long Island. The excited radio producer asked if he might come into the city to appear as a commentator for a live broadcast of the emerging *Doria–Stockholm* story. Frank was an expert on ocean liners, his favorite type of all ships. He agreed, decided to drive instead of taking his usual Long Island Railroad train, and all but left his home in pajamas. While driving, he would, as he thought, plan his remarks. But he realized that in the hurried, dramatic, excitement of the radio producer's phone call the names of the two disaster ships had not been revealed. He had absolutely no idea of which liners were involved. It was, after all, a half century or more before the current age of mobile phones and texting. For Frank, the forty-five minutes of preparation while driving in the deep dark of that summer's night was lost.

In the following days, Frank volunteered at the Italian Line's State Street offices in Lower Manhattan. He helped man phones and delivered coffee and donuts to overworked, distraught, deeply saddened Italian Line staff. He also joined them at the office windows, which overlooked Battery Park and the Upper Bay, as the *Stockholm* arrived. She sailed slowly, surrounded by tugs and press boats, but minus her bow. The Italian Line staff watched. They stared. Their eyes were focused in anger. Frank told me, 'They had daggers in their eyes. The *Stockholm* was the villain!'

Newspapers and television followed up for at least a week with further reports, recollections from survivors and tales from heroic rescue ships like the legendary *Ile de France* and the freighter *Cape Ann*. Rather quickly, *Life* magazine even rushed out an issue about salvaging the *Andrea Doria*. Could she be dragged to shore by huge chains? Could she be systematically pumped-out and slowly floated to the surface? Or, in deeper imagination, could she be filled with the likes of thousands of ping-pong balls and refloated? In fact, the Italians wanted nothing of salvage. In deepening silence, the company – both in New York and at its Genoa headquarters – slipped into total retreat on the subject of the *Andrea Doria*. Almost immediately, it was announced instead that a bigger, more luxurious replacement would be built – dubbed the 'super *Andrea Doria*' by one newspaper – and would be in service in less than four years. The Italians focused on the positive, the future, the continuing of its famed trans-Atlantic liner service.

The *Stockholm* went into its own kind of hiding. After landing her passengers, survivors and most of crew, she was towed stern-first by Moran tugs from Pier 97, south along the Hudson and over to the bottom end of the Brooklyn waterfront, to the Bethlehem Steel shipyard at 56th Street. Placed immediately into dry dock, the *Stockholm* would need serious surgery: four months of repairs and the replacement of her raked, ice-strengthened bow. Tucked in an inner floating dock, the *Stockholm* was not easily seen (or photographed) from, say, a passing ship or Staten Island ferry.

Being a well-known maritime expert and very friendly man, Frank Braynard had friends at Bethlehem Steel. One of them phoned in that late summer of 1956 and offered Frank a prized item: the original, 8-foot tall letter 'S' from the Swedish ship's bow. The item remained in Frank's extensive collection until 2007.

Under the good care of Grandfather Miller, I was an eleven-year-old schoolboy when, during one of our monthly walking tours of Manhattan, we ventured over to Grand Central station, the magnificent railway terminal located on East 42nd Street and in the shadows of the gleaming Chrysler Building. The visit had a special purpose: an 18-foot-long model of the 'finest Italian liner yet' was on display. My eyes widened, a big smile broke out and I studied almost every detail – the new flagship *Leonardo da Vinci* was Italy's replacement for the *Andrea Doria*. She was bigger, more modern and had a sleeker exterior appearance. She was, in a word, magnificent. That model later went home to Italy, was kept by the Italian Line and then was about to be discarded as Italian Line ended its passenger liner services in 1976/7. There were two great heroes, however – Maurizio Eliseo and Paolo Piccione; both of whom rescued the model, had it thoroughly restored (in faraway Russia, no less) and then offered it for public display.

In the summer of 1988, I arrived in Genoa and had a short stay before heading off on two Mediterranean cruises, both on Italian liners – the *Achille Lauro* and the *Ausonia*. While in a Genoa hotel, I came across a newspaper. A headline read 'Death Ship Arrives'. A small, all-white passenger ship had arrived and was to be converted and made over as a contemporary cruise ship. Then over forty years old, it was the former *Stockholm*. The 'villain' in 1956 was now an Italian ship.

In April 2001, I traveled to the Caribbean, to Montego Bay in Jamaica, to board a rather special cruise. It included three days in otherwise remote Cuba: two days in Havana and a day at a beach resort called the Isle of Youth. The ship was the specially chartered *Valtur Prima*, the former *Stockholm*. She had, however, been so completely rebuilt that there was very little trace of her earlier Scandinavian heritage. I searched all through the passenger areas. While using the ship's tenders, however, we would pass the knife-like bow. Upon looking closely, the slightly raised but very faint lettering was visible – it spelled *Stockholm*.

Five years later, in 2006, I was a board member of the Ocean Liner Museum, an on-going project then based at Lower Manhattan's South Street Seaport Museum. Along with a permanent exhibit, we offered periodic lectures and programs and decided to commemorate the fiftieth anniversary of the sinking of the *Andrea Doria*. There was a half-day exhibit of memorabilia, artifacts and photos of the Italian liner, as well as a series of talks. John Moyer talked of his various salvage efforts, others spoke about the Italian Line and its ships, and still others recalled personal memories of the tragedy. One lady traveled from New Jersey and spoke, often with high emotion. She was a teenager in 1956 and was sent by her family to begin a new life by living with relatives in America. Her parents brought her to Naples, where she boarded the *Andrea Doria*. She shared a four-berth room in tourist class and was looked after by the three older ladies sharing the same room. On the night of 25 July, she was suddenly awakened and told to hurry – the three ladies would take her to the lifeboats up on boat deck. She described the great commotion, the sense of the unknown and fear as the crowds of frantic passengers moved along stairwells and corridors. She was guided to a lifeboat, but then was deeply embarrassed. She was wearing only pajamas and slippers in front of a Catholic priest, who was joining the same lifeboat. That, she told us, was more upsetting than the drama unfolding with the ship itself. The ship already had a great list as she was herded into a lifeboat and then, in the dark of night, sent off to a rescue ship, the liner *Ile de France*. Seeing the ship sink the following morning was 'horrifying'. Later met by relatives at New York's Pier 88, she never forgot the *Andrea Doria*, or the sinking that night. Nightmares haunted her for years. Until that morning in 2006, she was never again able to board another ship, not even a harbor ferryboat.

2016 is the sixtieth anniversary of the *Andrea Doria* sinking. That number prompted this book, another look back. In addition, I have selected some other passenger-ship disasters, but not all. Many liners finish their days at the scrapyard, reduced to rubble, but some have had tragic, very sad endings. This is a record, beginning in 1942, of some of those passenger-ship disasters.

Bill Miller,
Summer 2016

Andrea Doria

As of July 2016, it has been sixty years. The *Andrea Doria* – a grand ocean liner given immortality, primarily for her tragic ending – rests on her starboard side in the cold waters off Nantucket Island. She is some 225 feet down, much diminished with time and erosion and, that relatively new dimension, global warming. She is still interesting and remains a lure to divers. Her mast and single funnel are long gone, disintegrated in that underwater grave, while the wheelhouse, bridge and upper decks have crumbled into watery decay. On 26 July 1956, the most glorious Italian liner of her time, the 29,000-ton *Andrea Doria*, sank after colliding with another passenger ship, Sweden's comparatively small 12,000-ton *Stockholm*.

The Italian Line was one of the Atlantic's most popular firms. They were noted for fine food, fine service and a certain happy atmosphere – 'a sort of "summer at sea" tone', reported one seasoned traveler of the 1950s period. 'After your talk on the great Atlantic liners yesterday [aboard the *Queen Mary 2*], I went back to my room and shed a few tears,' said Virginia Martinelli, a striking, elegant women with wonderful silver-gray hair who lives in Manhattan. She recalls,

> I well remember Pier 84. It was at the far end of 44th Street. I can still almost see it – the crowds, the luggage, those big yellow taxis. There was this sense of excitement. My parents were born in Italy and, in the 1950s and 60s, they visited family there every two or three years. I remember the onboard *bon voyage* parties, the champagne, the little sandwiches, the streamers at sailing and the sounds of the ship's whistle. It was a combination of feelings for me as a daughter and as an only child – I felt the excitement and the joy, but I also felt the sadness of seeing my father and mother departing and being away for as long as two or three months. They would not fly and so they crossed on those beautiful Italian liners, ships like the *Vulcania, Conte Biancamano, Giulio Cesare, Cristoforo Colombo, Leonardo da Vinci, Michelangelo* and *Raffaello*. There was a great spirit and an appeal to Italian Line back then – helpful stewards, charming pursers and some of the most handsome officers I'd ever seen. But, sometimes, my parents also sailed to or from Italy on the *Constitution* and *Independence*. They were very nice ships, very modern and up to date, but they did not have the same spirit or style of the Italian liners. Those ships sailed from Pier 84 as well. Once I remember seeing my parents off on the Italian Line and then meeting them on their return from Naples

aboard either the *Constitution* or *Independence*. In 1980, after my father had died, my mother flew to Italy for the very first time. She was all but terrified, clutching her rosary beads for the entire eight hours to Rome. By then, of course, there was no longer an Italian Line. So, a few tears. I miss my parents, I miss the ships, I miss those wonderful *bon voyage* sailings at Pier 84.

Italy had lost all but four of its great, pre-war liners. Renewal and rebuilding were the orders of the day in those early post-Second World War years of the late 1940s. The restored *Saturnia*, *Vulcania*, *Conte Biancamano* and *Conte Grande* needed assistance and new liners were commissioned. The first big pair were the 27,000-ton sister ships *Giulio Cesare* and *Augustus*, but these were aimed at the South Atlantic, at the booming Italy–Brazil–Argentina run. Tens of thousands of Italians alone were seeking new lives and greater economic opportunity in Latin America. Then came a pair for the North Atlantic – bigger, faster and more luxurious. They were named *Andrea Doria* and *Cristoforo Colombo*.

'The *Andrea Doria* and the *Cristoforo Colombo* introduced new concepts in design, had stylish, very modern interiors and used the best names in Italian art and decoration,' noted Maurizio Eliseo, one of Italy's finest maritime scholars and authors. 'It was said at the time [1952] that the *Andrea Doria* was a "ship built like an oil on canvas, with parts of the greatest artists coming together". Some of her artwork was, in fact, inspired by the Renaissance, the great master artists, and of course she was a symbol of another renaissance, the Italian maritime renaissance of the late 1940s and '50s. Alone, the *Andrea Doria* was a great symbol.'

The 700-foot-long *Andrea Doria* would cost $16.5 million to build, of which a quarter was contributed by the Italian government. The Italian Line itself was part of Finmare, the government-controlled group that managed four of Italy's biggest lines: Italian Line, Lloyd Triestino, Adriatica Line and Tirrenia Lines. The *Doria* was launched on 16 June 1951. During her sea trials in the fall of 1952, she reached a very impressive 25 knots as a top speed. She would therefore comfortably make 23 knots in regular. In the same year, the brilliant *United States* first appeared as well. Comparatively, she would average 33 knots in North Atlantic service, reached an astounding 43 knots during her sea trials and had as much as 241,000 horsepower. Nevertheless, the *Doria* was a very important ship and attracted great press attention on both sides of the Atlantic.

A three-class ship that could carry as many as 1,241 passengers (218 in first class, 320 cabin class and 703 tourist), the 23-knot, steam-turbine *Doria* was built at Genoa by the Ansaldo shipyard. She was commissioned in December 1952, beginning with a short cruise from Genoa to the western Mediterranean and out to the Canary Islands. Eliseo went on to comment,

> She was an outstanding ship when completed. Everyone was very pleased with her. She was, after all, the first North Atlantic liner built in Italy since the 1930s. She was also said to be very advanced. Her safety, for example, was assured, not only by the Italians, but by the Americans and British as well. She was actually said to be one of the safest ships afloat. More than a few publications went so far as to dub the new ship 'unsinkable'. Safety was paramount at the time for the Italians. They wanted especially to revive their fine shipbuilding reputation from before the war. Earlier, the Italian superliners *Rex* and *Conte di Savoia* [both completed in 1932] had been the very first passenger ships to comply with SOLAS [Safety Of Life At Sea] standards of 1929. The *Doria* complied with newer standards, amended in 1948.

The *Andrea Doria* was highly popular on the so-called 'Sunny Southern Route' – regularly sailing between Naples, Genoa, Cannes, Gibraltar and New York. She and the *Cristoforo Colombo*, added in the summer of 1954, maintained Italian Line's premier express service.

To many, the *Doria* as well as the *Cristoforo Colombo* were appraised from the start as two of the most beautiful-looking liners of the post-Second World War era. 'The *Andrea Doria* as well as her sister were yacht-like in appearance,' commented New York-based memorabilia dealer and ocean-liner collector Richard Faber. 'They were the most beautiful ships of the entire Italian Line post-war fleet. From stem to stern, they had perfect proportions.' Also based in New York, the late, noted architect Der Scutt added, 'The *Doria* and the *Colombo* may have been two of the most beautiful liners ever built. The uniformity of massing, splendid proportions and harmonious integration of parts was magnificent. The scale was just right. A building can have proper or poor scale; most designers do not know the importance of scale, nor how to achieve it. The Italians do it perfect!'

Following that introductory cruise from Genoa, the *Doria* had a brief turn in a Genoa shipyard for final checks and adjustments before setting off for New York on 14 January 1953. She reached Manhattan's Lower Bay nine days later. Fares for the maiden voyage included $525 for a single-bedded room with private bathroom in first class, $300 for a double with bath in cabin class and $200 for a berth in a quad down in tourist class and without private facilities. The crossing, while gala and celebratory, was, however, not without its troubles. 'Near the American coast, the liner was by hit by enormous waves that rolled her over 28 degrees and sent diners, tables and chairs into a scrambling heap in the main dining rooms,' reported the *New York Times*. 'The new liner was subjected to a test so severe that twenty of her 794 passengers were injured. The officers said the *Doria* had covered the 4,737 miles from Genoa to New York at an average speed of 22.97 knots despite the storm, which forced a reduction to 18 knots at one time.'

Tugs and spraying fireboats and buzzing helicopters welcomed the *Andrea Doria*. The mayor of New York City boarded in the Lower Bay and sailed with the new ship up to Pier 84. After docking at noon, the ship remained in port for seven days before departing for a seventeen-day cruise to the sunny West Indies. During her inaugural visit, the ship was the site of numerous receptions, luncheons and dinners for officials and members of the shipping and travel industries. On the day after her arrival, she was opened to the general public from one to five in the afternoon. Boarding fees were one dollar for adults and fifty cents for children, with proceeds going to the Travelers Aid Society. The only blemish for the new ship was spoken of quietly along the waterfront. It was said that, under certain conditions, the *Andrea Doria* had stability problems. She was said to be a 'fragile ship'.

The *Doria* had superb, often stunning, interiors, particularly in her first-class quarters. Former Italian Line executive Sal Scannella noted,

> Pre-war grandeur was supplanted with quiet, refined elegance coming on the scene as Italian post-war culture was enjoying worldwide popularity and acclaim. The *Andrea Doria* and her sister symbolized the best in contemporary Italian art and design. Italian post-war high fashion was found through the first and cabin class. The *Doria*'s interiors caused a minor sensation. In many ways, the *Doria* was the most decoratively daring post-war Atlantic liner. Many famous architects contributed to her interiors, including Gio Ponti, who considered the *Doria* his maritime masterpiece. Overall, the *Doria*'s style was a blend of dramatic, modern art and furniture with strong styling and bold themes which heralded a new more conventional style.

Scannella, who crossed several times on Italian liners, added,

> There was indeed great romance in the Italian Line and its ships. 'Arriverderci Roma', 'Al Di La' or perhaps 'Volare' being played

by the Italian quartet as you sip Campari in an alta moda lounge designed by Pulitzer or Ponti. A poolside luncheon of melone coin prosciutto and spaghetti alla putanesca. The umbrellas and the sunshine of the lido deck as you sail the sunny southern route eastbound or westbound. Evocative aromas of pesto, garlic, espresso, linoleum polish and sun-warmed teak decks.

There was also the wonderful noontime signal countdown, the Carosello Napolitano crew show, the elegance, the luxurious ballrooms, the Murano chandeliers, the glorious food and the impeccable service, the Italian ambiance. I could go on forever.

But the fates were cruel to the glorious, 29,000-ton *Doria*. On a foggy summer night, 25 July 1956, she was rammed off Nantucket Island by another liner, the *Stockholm*. The Swedish ship was far smaller, however, at 12,500 tons. The New York-bound *Andrea Doria* was mortally wounded. While the badly damaged Swede limped back to New York, the abandoned pride of Italy rolled over on her side and sank in the early daylight of the next morning. She was gone, over fifty souls had perished, and a long court battle over responsibility followed. It was, in fact, never settled.

The *Andrea Doria* left Genoa on 17 July, a normal, but well-booked, summer season crossing to New York. En route, the seas were calm and the ship made good speed. Clear skies with warm sunshine gave way to a foggy night, however, on 25 July 1956, the day before the liner was due in New York. Among the 1,708 passengers and crew aboard, the first-class passenger list included Hollywood actress Ruth Roman, several American politicians, a pair of European ballet dancers and the mayor of Philadelphia. With the evening fog, her captain began to worry that he might have to reduce speed and therefore delay her scheduled arrival at Pier 84, closely scheduled by the home office for eight the next morning.

Meanwhile, at eleven o'clock that morning, the Swedish American liner *Stockholm* had left Pier 97 – thirteen New York City blocks north of the Italian Line terminal – on an eastbound crossing to Copenhagen and Gothenburg. Thirty minutes later, French Line's *Ile de France* cast off, also on an eastward passage, to Plymouth and Le Havre. Together with the *Andrea Doria*, all three ships would, quite unexpectedly, have a fateful meeting later that night.

At eleven o'clock that night, in thick fog off Nantucket, the officers onboard the *Doria* noticed the lights of another ship. Radar had not yet been perfected, and the first pip of that other ship was miscalculated and quickly came much closer. She was believed to be a small freighter. In fact, it was the *Stockholm*. The two liners were traveling at a combined speed of 40 knots (or 46 miles per hour) and therefore moving at the rate of approximately one mile per minute. At 11.21 p.m., the *Stockholm* materialized out of the fog and rammed into the *Doria*. The stricken ship abruptly and dramatically lurched over to port and then righted. Passengers and crew heard the sounds of a grinding crash, and some saw the bright lights of the *Stockholm* through the *Doria*'s windows and portholes. The Swedish ship's reinforced bow was like a dagger piercing the larger Italian. She cut 40 feet into the *Doria*'s hull, just below the bridge, created a jagged hole like an inverted pyramid that extended from below the waterline up to B Deck. It was a mortal wound. The two liners were entangled together for a short time until movement tore them apart. Fifty-five feet of the *Stockholm*'s foredeck and bow were folded and mangled into a tangled mass of steel. The *Doria* sent out an immediate SOS and began the starboard list from which she would never recover. With her fuel tanks all but empty (and that 'stability issue' noted from her maiden voyage), she had very little ballast and was very fragile. The two ships were some 45 miles south of Nantucket Island, in a sea lane known as the 'Crossroads of the Atlantic' because of its very busy shipping patterns. No fewer than eleven US Coast Guard cutters were immediately dispatched to sea following the first calls for help from the stricken Italian liner. 'The *Andrea Doria* could also have caught fire with the great impact of the collision with the *Stockholm*,' observed Captain Ed Squire, 'but fortunately this was not an added problem in the tragedy.'

It was soon realized that the badly damaged *Stockholm* was in no danger of sinking, and so began to assist the badly damaged *Doria*. Below decks on the Italian ship, crewmen struggled quickly with flooding and furiously tried to pump out the floods of invading Atlantic water. Meanwhile, deck crews worked promptly to rig rope ladders and nets so passengers could clamber down the ship's sides and reach waiting lifeboats. All of the port-side lifeboats were useless because of the severe, ever-increasing list to starboard. The *Doria*'s electrical system fortunately continued to work, along with the huge boat-deck emergency searchlights. An onlooker reported, 'Lighted up and with searchlights acting as beacons for lifeboats, the *Stockholm* and other, soon-to-arrive rescue ships, the stricken *Andrea Doria* was obviously doomed. She was already listing badly.'

Passengers slid down ropes – off the stern, off the bow, off the quarter. Small children and the elderly were carried. The steady relay of lifeboats, while largely successful, was frequently a clumsy affair and, all throughout the night, the often unwieldy lifeboats were manned not by seamen, but by cooks, waiters and bellhops. The *Doria*'s whistle moaned continuously – 'Her death rattle,' as one survivor called it. A small armada of rescue ships began to gather around the liner as passengers and crew fled for safety and sought assistance and rescue. For a time, radio traffic between the rescue ships, as well as from shore, became overloaded and confusing. By the first daylight, the *Doria* was keeled well over to starboard and was all but fully abandoned. The last passengers had been removed by five o'clock in the morning, over five hours after the collision. Only Captain Calamai and a few officers remained aboard, hoping that the stricken liner might somehow be saved. Below, the pumps still throbbed as tons of seawater was pumped overboard. It was all to no avail – the *Doria* was doomed.

At six in the morning, the Coast Guard cutter *Hornblower* eased alongside the sinking liner. There was no hope. The captain and his last remaining officers and crew were taken off. 'Both Moran Towing and another New York firm, the big salvage company Merritt, Chapman & Scott, were called during the night by the Italian Line. They discussed towing the liner and then beaching it, perhaps on the shores of Nantucket,' recalled Captain Ed Squire. 'But there was not enough time. She was sinking far too quickly. Furthermore, with the great list, she might have turned over completely if a tow was attempted. Realistically, the *Andrea Doria* could not have withstood the stress of a towline.'

Captain Raffaele Gavino was aboard another Italian Line passenger ship, the *Augustus*, then sailing off the West African coast and bound for ports along the east coast of South America on the tragic night of 25 July,

I was second mate on watch on the bridge when the captain of the *Augustus* arrived on the bridge to tell us that the *Andrea Doria*, our flagship, had been in a serious collision off the coast of New England and that she was in great danger. But we were assured that she was slowly headed for the coast, to be grounded. But a few hours later, the captain returned and, with tears in his eyes, gave us the very sad news. The *Andrea Doria* had sunk. It was very, very emotional for all of us. Later, we advised the passengers and crew onboard the *Augustus*.

With the *Stockholm* still waiting nearby, the drama was nearing its dramatic, very tragic end by nine o'clock in the morning. The summer sun was shining on the stricken liner. Silent passengers, the captain, his officers and crew watched transfixed, some as if stunned, as the abandoned liner – with her huge funnel, outer decks and three swimming pools clearly visible – was in her final hour.

In chronicling the worst ocean-liner disaster of its time, journalist Edward F. Oliver wrote, 'The *Andrea Doria* rolled bottom up, thrust her glistening propellers into the sunlight and then plunged to the ocean's floor. Her voyage had ended.' The US Coast Guard cutter *Evergreen* flashed the official obituary to the world: 'SS *Andrea Doria* sank in 225 feet of water at 10.09 a.m.' The cutter marked the grave with a floating tombstone: a yellow buoy. In the final totals, 1,662 were saved, fifty-two were lost – forty-six from the *Doria* and six from the *Stockholm*. Soon afterward, the ships that stood by – kept the 'death watch' – disbanded and headed mostly to New York.

'The sinking of the *Andrea Doria* holds special memories of many ocean liner historians and enthusiasts,' added Der Scutt. 'Her tragedy was like losing one of your beloved children. It had contributed so much to the love of ships and now the *Andrea Doria* was gone. The Italians strove for high authority, fantasy and symbolism with the *Doria* – and now she was gone!'

Sad, humiliated and almost disgraced, indeed the villain to many, the badly damaged *Stockholm* dragged itself back to New York, to Pier 97, where her voyage had begun the day before. She was the last of a virtual caravan of rescue ships to New York harbor. The French liner *Ile de France* was first, with 758 survivors; then the freighter *Cape Ann*, with 129; the US government transport *Pvt William H Thomas*, 158, and then the Navy destroyer USS *Edward H Allen*, 76. The wounded *Stockholm* arrived with 533 survivors. She crept through the western Atlantic waters at reduced speed to protect her forward bulkhead and mangled bow. Three Coast Guard cutters accompanied her just in case there were further problems. Reporters, photographers and journalists were aboard tugs and hired craft to meet the rescue ships, especially the *Stockholm*, in the Lower Bay of New York harbor. Anxious reporters yelled questions to survivors, mostly passengers, who lined the decks of these returning ships. It was the biggest news story of the day and everyone wanted stories and especially a reasoning, even a blame, for the tragic collision. Early reports were that the *Stockholm* was damaged beyond repair. How could she be repaired?

At first, the *Stockholm* waited at Pier 97, small and shadowed and seemingly hidden by the pier's green-colored shed. Swedish American Line had the good fortune to hear that New York-based Bethlehem

Steel Shipyard could repair the ship and do the job, all rather quickly in approximately four months, in their nearby Brooklyn yard. The *Stockholm* was towed by Moran tugs stern-first along the Hudson and over to the Bethlehem yard at the lower end of the Brooklyn waterfront, at the foot of 56th Street. The comparatively small Swedish liner would occupy the yard's big dry dock, one normally used by the likes of the 29,000-ton sisters *Constitution* and *Independence*. The wrecked bow was cleared and the bow section completely rebuilt, allowing the ship's return to service by early December.

Margaret Hall recalls,

> My husband was in the US Army and was posted to Germany. We were finally coming home, aboard the troopship *General Butner*, sailing from Bremerhaven to Brooklyn, when we hit a thick fog. I asked a ship's officer if ships could collide with one another in such a fog. He said it was very unlikely and that radar greatly reduced the possibility. The very next day we heard that the *Andrea Doria* sank after colliding with the *Stockholm*. The collision occurred in fog. We were so surprised – it was shocking news! When we finally landed in Brooklyn, we berthed next to a shipyard. The *Stockholm* was already there but without a bow. The front of that ship was a horrifying sight – it was one big gash.

The legendary *Ile de France*, which was 40 miles from the collision scene and steaming toward Europe, reversed course after receiving the SOS. She arrived with her twin funnels floodlit and her name in neon letters. She became a modern-day hero – 'the valiant ship', as she was dubbed – and was later given the Gallant Ship Award by the US Coast Guard. In recent years, the plaque was in in the French Line archives stored in Le Havre.

Within a month, newspaper and magazine articles hinted of plans to salvage the *Doria*. One ambitious report was that huge chains would be affixed to the hull and it would then be dragged near the shoreline, pumped out and refloated. Another was that a fleet of fifteen to twenty tugs would drag the wreck to shallow waters. Perhaps the most fanciful was the plan to fill the hull with a huge number of ping-pong balls and thereby refloat the ship. Nothing came to pass, of course, and instead the Italian Line abandoned the wreckage to underwriters soon after final investigations were complete. The *Andrea Doria* was barely, if ever, mentioned again by the Italian Line.

'It was really a national funeral when the *Doria* was lost,' noted Maurizio Eliseo. 'It was like seeing the dream of post-war Italy turn into a nightmare. In Genoa, people cried in the streets, others stood weeping outside Italian Line headquarters and badly depressed dockers even refused to load ships. Within two days, the Italian Line, attempting to revive spirits, announced their plans for the *Leonardo da Vinci*. She would be bigger, faster, more beautiful, even more gorgeous.'

Extensive, but very confidential, inquiries and hearings began in August and continued into the following year. In the end, the total compensation amounted to $48 million, but no precise responsibility was determined. Years later, it was revealed that the Italians actually assumed more responsibility. The final investigation was finally dropped at the mutual consent of the Italian and Swedish American lines. The Italians were especially anxious to restore their good image while, complicating matters further, the Swedes were building a new flagship, the 23,000-ton *Gripsholm*, at the Ansaldo shipyard in Genoa, at the time. 'It had all become quite sensitive,' remembered Captain Squire. The disaster did lead, however, to greatly increased radar navigation training for ships' officers. The *Stockholm* would sail for the Swedish American Line for another three years, until 1959; the *Andrea Doria* would be replaced by the *Leonardo da Vinci*, which had its debut in four years, in July 1960.

Forty years after the collision and sinking, in the mid '90s, the *Doria* was still a very topical ship – and something of a favorite in ship buff circles. 'She's hotter than ever [fall 1996],' according to Richard Faber, a New York City-based maritime memorabilia dealer and himself a specialist collector of the *Andrea Doria*. He went on,

> She is a famous liner linked to a famous tragedy. But the question remained: how could it have happened to a modern liner and in the age of radar? It was, quite obviously, the carelessness of man. More and more, collectors are fascinated with ships of disaster, especially liners of disaster. Of course, the *Titanic* is of the greatest interest, but in ways the *Doria* has become the modern-day *Titanic*.

By 2006, fifty years after the tragedy, the wreckage of the *Andrea Doria* was deteriorating at an increasing speed, possibly due to the effects of global warming on the seawater. Her funnel and upper decks are gone, disintegrated down to the Promenade Deck area. Over forty divers had been lost to that date in their attempts to reach and explore the sunken liner. A lure to countless divers, remnants from the ship – from dining room china to medicine bottles from the ship's hospital to notes of Italian lire – have been retrieved. Even the statue of Andrea

Doria has been removed. After twenty-six years, in 1982, a lifeboat washed ashore on Staten Island, and a weathered life jacket sold for $7,000 on the memorabilia market.

Postscript: the former *Stockholm*

Sixty-seven years old. In June 2015, I arrived by cruise ship in Iceland. Docked just astern of us in Reykjavik was the *Azores*. The *Azores*, some onlookers on deck asked? Well, while looking modern and in very good condition as well, the 15,000-ton ship has in fact had a long and varied history. She started life as the *Stockholm* – yes, the infamous Swedish liner that rammed the *Andrea Doria* on the night of 25 July 1956. Repaired and given a new bow, the *Stockholm* was sold to the East German government in 1960. She became the Communist Party workers' cruise ship *Volkerfreundschaft* – translating to 'International Friendship". The very first cruise ship of its kind, good party members who were nominated for being productive and who passed through no fewer than eight security checkpoints, sailed from Rostock to nearby Soviet ports, Black Sea resorts in Soviet Romania and Bulgaria and – once a year – across the Atlantic to Castro's Cuba. She was sold again in 1985, becoming a moored hostel for Asian refugees at Oslo.

Coincidentally, the Italians bought her in 1989, had her towed to Genoa (where newspapers recalled her history and dubbed her 'the death ship') and then totally rebuilt and even re-engined the then forty-plus-year-old ship. She did further cruising as the 600-bed *Italia Prima* and then *Valtur Prima*. I cruised on her in April 1991 – sailing out of Montego Bay to Mexico, Grand Cayman and – most unusually – two ports in Cuba: an overnight in Havana and a day at a beach resort named the Isle of Youth. Onboard, she was very contemporary, shiny and modern. There was barely a trace of her earlier heritage. She was owned by the Portuguese for a period of time, though cruising on charter to the UK-based Cruise & Maritime Voyages. By 2016, though, she went off on another charter, being renamed *Astoria*.

The *Andrea Doria* fitting-out at Genoa in 1952. (Maurizio Eliseo Collection)

Resting between voyages at Pier 84, at the foot of West 44th Street. (ALF Collection)

Departing Genoa. (ALF Collection)

The Gallant
new
Cristoforo Colombo

500 years to build this ship . . . do Vinci, Michelangelo, Titian, Cellini . . . you'll feel their spirit and see the mark of their immortal minds in every detail of this great new ship.

You'll see it in the smouldering colors of her mosaic tile and the intricate beauty of her tapestries and in-

laid woods. You'll feel it in the soft luxury of Milanese fabrics and Florentine leathers. You'll hear it in the bell-like ring of Venetian crystal and the courteous tons of a Roman steward. She is the fulfillment of the rich Renaissance tradition, five centuries old. She is the gallant new *Cristoforo Colombo*.

See your Travel Agent or

Italian Line

"ITALIA" Società di Navigazione—Genova

Battery Park Bldg., 24 State Street, New York 4, Tel.: Digby 4-0800

CHICAGO • SEATTLE • PORTLAND, ORE.
LOS ANGELES • SAN FRANCISCO

CRISTOFORO COLOMBO • ANDREA DORIA EXPRESS SERVICE ON THE SUNNY SOUTHERN ROUTE • 6 DAYS to GIBRALTAR • 8 DAYS to NAPLES • 9 DAYS to CANNES and GENOA
SATURNIA • VULCANIA • CONTE BIANCAMANO TO AZORES • PORTUGAL • NORTH AFRICA • GIBRALTAR • SPAIN • MAJORCA • FRANCE • ITALY • SICILY

HOLIDAY/SEPTEMBER

The Sunny Southern Route: An advertisement dated 1954 heralding the maiden voyage of the *Cristoforo Colombo*, sister ship to *Andrea Doria*. (Holiday Magazine)

Busy decor: The Zodiac Suite aboard the *Andrea Doria*. (Maurizio Eliseo Collection)

A poster marking the maiden cruise of the
Andrea Doria, departing from Genoa on
23 December 1952. (Norman Knebel Collection)

Modern Italian decor: first class aboard the *Andrea Doria*. (ALF Collection)

Sisters meeting: the *Cristoforo Colombo* (left) and *Andrea Doria* meet at Genoa. (ALF Collection)

Rare occasion in December 1954: five Italian Line passenger ships are together at Genoa – *Andrea Doria* (top), *Conte Grande, Vulcania, Giulio Cesare* and *Cristoforo Colombo*. (Author's Collection)

Winter weather: The *Andrea Doria* arriving at Pier 84 for the first time on a gray January morning in 1953. (ALF Collection)

The *Andrea Doria* and her sister ship were among the most beautiful post-war Atlantic liners. (ALF Collection)

By daylight on 26 July, the mighty *Doria* has a severe list. (ALF Collection)

All of the ship's port side lifeboats were useless due to the severe list to starboard from the start. (Cronican-Arroyo Collection)

The transport *Pvt William H. Thomas* is among the rescue ships and waits in the hazy distance. (Cronican-Arroyo Collection)

The *Andrea Doria* is abandoned by the early daylight of 26 July. (Cronican-Arroyo Collection)

The outer decks are empty, the great liner deserted. (Cronican-Arroyo Collection)

Her last gasps of life. (Cronican-Arroyo Collection)

One of the last views – the pride of the Italian Line rolls over and sinks. (Cronican-Arroyo Collection)

In better, happier times: The *Stockholm* is on the left in this view from the harbor in Gothenburg, Sweden. Another Swedish passenger ship, the *Patricia* of Swedish Lloyd, is on the left. (Albert Wilhelmi Collection)

A colorized view of the battered Swedish liner. (ALF Collection)

Another view of
the badly damaged
Stockholm.
(Moran Towing &
Transportation Co.)

In the Hudson River,
just off Pier 94
and about to berth
at Pier 97. (ALF
Collection)

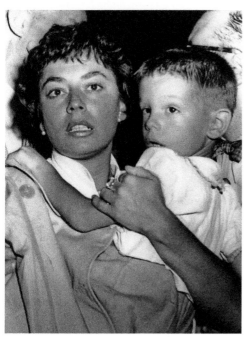

Actress Ruth Roman has been reunited with
her young son at Pier 88. Mother and child
were separated during the evacuation of the
Andrea Doria. (Author's Collection)

Another Italian liner, the *Conte Grande* was hurriedly moved from the South American to the New York run to cope with the need for passenger accommodation following the loss of the *Andrea Doria*. (ALF Collection)

Collectibles from the *Andrea Doria*. (Richard Romano Collection)

Collecting items from the *Andrea Doria*
is very popular. These items belong
to New Jersey-based collector Richard
Romano.

John Moyer with Gambone Panel recovered from the ship's Winter Garden Lounge. (Bill Campbell)

Gambone Panel cleaned and restored. Guido Gambone's works were heavily influenced by his friend Pablo Picasso. (John Moyer Collection)

Three sizes of first-class cups and saucers (John Moyer Collection)

Normandie

Dreamboat destroyed! She was said to be the most magnificent Atlantic liner of all time. Commissioned in 1935, the 82,799-grt *Normandie* was the pride of France, the flagship of the French Line and the most luxurious art deco liner ever. Carrying as many as 1,972 passengers in three classes, the $60 million *Normandie* was, for a time, also the world's largest and fastest liner. Used on the North Atlantic, crossing between Le Havre, Southampton and New York, she developed a huge reputation – for luxury, for service and certainly for food. Dinners in first class had as many as 325 items listed in the menu, for example, and were taken in a dining room that was longer than the Hall of Mirrors at Versailles and decorated with bronze, hammered glass and Lalique. Unfortunately, she sailed commercially for only a little more than four years, until August 1939, when she was laid up at New York's Pier 88. War would soon start in Europe and the ship would never sail again. Seized by the United States in December 1941, she was to be converted to a high-capacity (15,000-plus) Allied troopship, being renamed USS *Lafayette*. The conversion was done at Pier 88, under urgent and hurried circumstances, and then resulted in tragedy. On 9 February 1942, sparks from a workman's acetylene torch ignited a fire that, fanned by New York's winter winds, spread throughout the entire ship. The fire was serious, but it was the firefighting that spelled the ship's end – the 1,028-ft long ship was so overloaded with water that it capsized on the morning of 10 February. The ship was soon deemed beyond repair, underwent a long and expensive salvage and then, in November 1943, the remaining hull was towed off (to a Brooklyn pier) to await the end of the war. It was declared surplus in 1946 and later sold (for $161,000) to Port Newark, New Jersey scrappers.

The great *Normandie* at Pier 88, at the time of her maiden arrival in June 1935. (Author's Collection)

On a cold winter afternoon, 9 February 1942, fire sweeps through the 1,028-foot-long *Normandie* at Pier 88. (Cronican-Arroyo Collection)

Firemen battle the blaze and, among other entries, go aboard the blazing liner at the bow. (Cronican-Arroyo Collection)

Mayor Fiorello La Guardia was among those who arrived at Pier 88 at the time of the fire. (Cronican-Arroyo Collection)

As the great liner began to list to the port side, she yanked gangways from Pier 88. (Author's Collection)

On her side, the
Normandie looked sad,
even grotesque. (ALF
Collection)

Motorists on the
West Side Highway
slowed to see the
capsized *Normandie*.
(Cronican-Arroyo
Collection)

Canvas life rafts line the starboard side of the
former French flagship. They would never be
used. (Cronican-Arroyo Collection)

With her superstructure removed, American servicemen watch as the liner is gradually pumped out. (Cronican-Arroyo Collection)

A lone sailor stands guard at the outer end of Pier 88 as the *Normandie* rests on its port side. (Cronican-Arroyo Collection)

In a rare color view, demolition of the *Normandie*'s funnels and upper decks has begun. (ALF Collection)

Hudson River water pours out of the liner. (Richard Weiss Collection)

In the shadows of a November day, the *Normandie* passes the Statue of Liberty on her way to the big, 1,100-foot-long graving dock at Bayonne, New Jersey. (ALF Collection)

Cast off: the *Normandie* spends her final years, empty and forgotten at the Columbia Street pier in Brooklyn. Wartime ships crowd the docks behind, in the Erie Basin. (ALF Collection)

Georgic

Some salvage efforts were extraordinary! Built for Britain's White Star Line (and later operated by a combined Cunard-White Star), the 27,759-grt *Georgic* was completed in 1932 for service to New York from Liverpool and later London. Becoming a troopship in 1940, however, she went on voyages elsewhere. She was bombed, set afire and badly damaged during a Nazi air attack at Port Tewfik, Egypt on 14 July 1941. The 711-foot-long ship seemed to be beyond repair, but the urgency of war created one of the longest salvage efforts ever. Towed to Port Sudan, Karachi, Bombay and finally all the way to Belfast, it took over three years to repair and restore the ship. Back to trooping, she was refitted as a migrant and low-fare passenger ship in the late forties and endured until scrapped in 1956.

The 711-foot-long *Georgic*. (Richard Faber Collection)

Rex

Some disasters involving ocean liners were avoidable. The 51,062-grt *Rex* was the pride of Italy when the 2,358-berth liner was commissioned in 1932. She also ranked as the world's fastest liner for two years (1933–35). Laid-up in 1940 due to the Second World War, the *Rex* was kept in obscure lay-up, first at Bari on the Adriatic and later in a backwater bay near Trieste. Even though Italy had already fully surrendered, British aircraft bombed the 880-foot-long ship on 8 September 1944. A fire from end to end, she later capsized in shallow water. Unfortunately beyond economic repair, the senseless loss finished with the ship subject to a long demolition, from 1947 until 1958.

A near tragedy: During a fierce eastern Atlantic gale, the 936-foot former German liner *Europa*, by then in French hands as the renamed *Liberte*, was ripped from her moorings at Le Havre. The liner rammed the wreckage of a sunken liner, the *Paris*, and then all but capsized completely. Fortunately, the 51,000-grt ship was righted and, but for a time, rested on the harbor bottom. (Author's Collection)

The *Liberte*'s lower decks were completely flooded. The wreckage of the *Paris* lies behind. The *Liberte* was later raised and repaired. (Author's Collection)

Wilhelm Gustloff

Horrific tragedy! The Hitler regime was planning as many as ten 'Strength Through Joy' cruise liners in the late thirties and early forties. Only two were actually built, the first being the 25,484-grt, 1,465-passenger *Wilhelm Gustloff*. Created by the Nazi Party's German Labor Front, the plan was for propaganda cruises – less affluent Germans could cruise through a process created by the Nazis. The *Gustloff* saw less than two years of this service before being sent, in November 1940, to serve as a moored accommodation ship in German-occupied Gdynia in Poland. The 684-foot-long ship would not sail again until near the end of the war, on 30 January 1945. Overloaded with an estimated 6,100 evacuees, mostly refugees and wounded, she was headed for German waters when she was torpedoed by a Soviet sub in the cold, ice-filled waters of the Baltic. The ship sank in forty minutes. Only 904 were rescued; an estimated 5,200 perished. It was ranked as the worst single worst maritime tragedy of all time.

The Nazi cruise ship *Wilhelm Gustloff*, seen at Hamburg; it was later the setting of the worst maritime tragedy to date. (Author's Collection)

Cap Arcona

More, almost unimaginable horror! The 27,560-ton *Cap Arcona* was the German queen of the South Atlantic. Built in 1927, she was their largest, fastest and finest liner on the run from Hamburg to Rio de Janeiro, Santos, Montevideo and Buenos Aires. A grand looking three-stacker belonging to the Hamburg-South America Line, she was one of Germany's most famous liners in the 1930s. Like the *Wilhelm Gustloff*, she was used as an accommodation ship at Nazi-occupied beginning in 1940. She would not put to sea in over four years. The 676-footer was reactivated in January 1945 for evacuation voyages – the Nazis were fleeing from the so-called eastern territories. The *Cap Arcona* made three such voyages and in April 1945 was overloaded with 5,000 prisoners from the Neuengamme concentration camp and another 1,000 guards, soldiers and crew. There were over 6,000 onboard: on 3 May, in the Bay of Lubeck, the liner was sighted by British aircraft, bombed and set afire. Panic broke out onboard and the ship capsized. Lying on her side and not far from shore, the disaster claimed some 5,000 lives. The death of the concentration camp prisoners was made all the more tragic – they would have been liberated during the collapse of Nazi Germany days later.

Cap Arcona at Hamburg. (ALF Collection)

Magdalena

Early tragedy! Belonging to London-headquartered Royal Mail Lines, the 17,547-grt *Magdalena* was the company's new, post-war replacement liner for their UK–South America service. The fanfare and excitement soon turned to loss, however. During the 570-foot-long ship's maiden voyage, on 25 April 1949, the liner ran aground on a rocky coast near Rio de Janeiro. The passengers and most crew were taken off, and the ship later refloated. But during the tow, the ship broke in two – the forepart sank and the aft section became useless, having to be scrapped locally.

The *Magdalena* loading in the London Docks.

Empress of Canada

Tragedy on a quiet Sunday: built in 1928 as the *Duchess of Richmond*, this Canadian Pacific liner became the *Empress of Canada* after the Second World War. The 20,325-ton ship was used on the Liverpool–Montreal run, carrying as many as 700 passengers, and was being refitted on 25 January 1953 in preparation of an especially busy coronation year on the North Atlantic. The 600-foot-long liner caught fire and then capsized against her Liverpool berth. Badly damaged and then found to be beyond repair, she underwent a long salvage before being towed off to Italy and the scrapyard in 1954.

Following a fire along the Liverpool docks, the *Empress of Canada* has capsized after being overloaded with firefighters' waters. Notice how the twin funnels and masts have bent. (Author's Collection)

With her upper decks removed (like the *Normandie*), the 600-foot-long *Empress of Canada* is being righted. (Author's Collection)

Another tragedy: The Danish combination passenger-cargo liner, the fifty-passenger *Erria*, caught fire off Astoria, Oregon, on 20 December 1951. The ship was later towed to Europe and repaired. (ALF Collection)

In February 1957, the Norwegian America Line's 16,844-grt *Oslofjord* slipped off the blocks in a floating dry dock at the Bethlehem Steel Shipyard in Hoboken, New Jersey. The 577-foot-long liner might have been lost. (Hoboken Historical Museum)

In fog outside New York harbor, on 1 March 1959, the big American liner *Constitution* was traveling too fast and cut the Norwegian tanker *Jalanta* in two. Fortunately, both sections of the tanker remained afloat and were later re-joined. (Moran Towing & Transportation Co.)

Dara

Terrorism at sea: this small, 5,000-grt passenger ship belonged to the British India Steam Navigation Company Limited, but never sailed in British waters. Instead, carrying up to 1,028 passengers (including 950 in deck class), the *Dara* traded on the Bombay–Persian Gulf local service. On 8 April 1961, the 1948-built ship made international headlines: a terrorist bomb exploded onboard and the ship caught fire. In all, 238 passengers and crew were lost. The badly burned ship itself was later placed under tow, but then sank on 10 April.

Burning badly: a terrorist bomb has destroyed the 5,000-grt *Dara* in April 1961. (British India Steam Navigation Co. Ltd)

The badly burned superstructure of British India's *Dara*. (British India Steam Navigation Co. Ltd)

Bianca C

Fire in the Caribbean: intended to be the *Marechal Petain*, but later, in 1949, completed as the *La Marseillaise* for France's Messageries Maritimes, she was the largest liner on the colonial run between Marseilles and French Indochina. After a rather short career, however, the 18,247-ton ship was sold to the Swiss-owned Arosa Line for trans-Atlantic service as the *Arosa Sky*. This phase was brief as well – in 1959, the 592-foot-long liner changed hands again, going to Italy's Costa Line and becoming the *Bianca C*. Used for cruising and Genoa–West Indies line service, she suffered from a malady common to French-built passenger ships: fire. On 24 October 1961, the 1,230-bed ship caught fire off St George, Granada, burned furiously and then later heeled over and sank.

The handsome Costa Line cruise ship *Bianca C* departing from New York in December 1959. (Costa Line)

Lakonia

Holiday tragedy! She was one of Holland's most famous and best-loved ships, and had one of the longest names to ever go to sea. Built in 1930, the *Johan van Oldenbarnevelt* was built by the Nederland Line for the East Indies colonial trade. The 20,314-grt liner did thirty-two years of service with the Dutch until she was sold, in 1962, to join the Greek Line and become their cruise ship *Lakonia*. Her last deployment: cruises from Southampton, England. During the holiday cruise of 1963, the voyage ended in tragedy. On 22 December, off Madeira, the 609-foot-long ship caught fire. Chaos among the passengers and crew followed, along with mishaps relating to evacuation and lifeboats. 128 perished – 95 passengers and 33 crew. Still burning, the ship was later placed under tow, but then sank on the 29th.

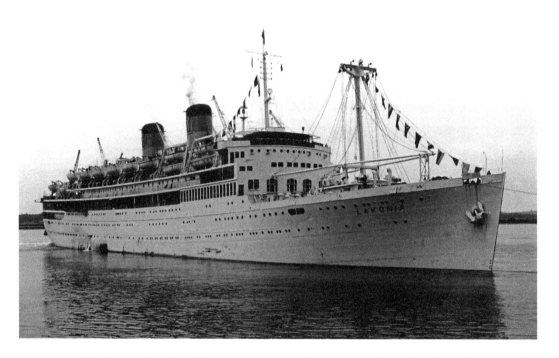

Dressed in flags and arriving from a cruise at Southampton, Greek Line's *Lakonia* became a ship of holiday disaster. (Roger Sherlock)

Once crowded with happy and relaxed passengers, the aft decks and the pool area of the *Lakonia* are abandoned. (ALF Collection)

In fog outside New York harbor, on 26 November 1964, the 25,320-grt, outbound *Shalom* – the new flagship of the Israeli merchant marine – rammed and sank the tanker *Stolt Dagali*. The liner returned to Pier 32 and, in unusual fashion, berthed stern first. (ALF Collection)

Yarmouth Castle

The dilemmas of aged tonnage! The small, 5,000-ton, 350-passenger sister ships *Yarmouth Castle* and *Yarmouth* were not untypical of cruise ships sailing in the 1950s and '60s. They were old, tired, past their best. They were also overpainted, worn out and, most likely, less than safe. Both were built in 1927 as 'mini liners' for the short-distance American intercoastal trade. In their later, final years, both ships cruised from Miami, then an infant cruise port and today the world's busiest. The *Yarmouth Castle* was making three- and four-night cruises over to Nassau twice a week until tragedy struck on 13 November 1965. After midnight, she caught fire while at sea. Poor seamanship, chaos and confusion followed and the blaze spread quickly – many passengers never left their cabins. Rescue ships hurried to the site and one, the *Bahama Star*, pulled alongside. An officer onboard reported, 'We could feel the heat of the blaze aboard the *Yarmouth Castle*. She was an inferno!' Abandoned and still burning, the old ship sank hours later, just before daybreak.

Viking Princess

On 8 April 1966, and with subsequent headline-making news, the cruise ship *Viking Princess* caught fire and burned out off Cuba. The 12,000-ton ship was on a Caribbean cruise at the time. Captain Klaus Schacht was then serving aboard the freighter *Cap Norte*, a West German vessel, and raced to the rescue. 'We rescued passengers and crew, but some of the crew were quite notorious. They seemed more interested with the monies and other valuables in the ship's safe.'

The fire started in the 17-knot ship's engine room and spread quickly. An order to abandon ship was ordered quickly and, along with the *Cap Norte*, two other freighters – the *Chungking Victory* and *Navigator* – rushed to the rescue. The *Navigator* did added duty: she towed the blistered, wrecked *Viking Princess* to Port Royal in Jamaica. Sadly, she had to be written-off as a complete loss and was later towed to Bilbao in Spain for scrapping.

The *Viking Princess* had been a French passenger-cargo ship, the *Lavoisier*, owned by a now long-vanished company called Chargeurs Reunis. A 537-foot-long ship, she was built at St Nazaire, France and completed in the summer of 1950. She and a sister, the *Claude Bernard*, carried lots of cargo and some 450 passengers (divided between first and third class) on the long-haul run from northern Europe to the east coast of South America – from the likes of Hamburg and Le Havre to Rio, Santos, Montevideo and Buenos Aires. In little more than a decade, however, she was sold to Italian buyers, who rebuilt her totally as the 600-passenger cruise ship *Riviera Prima*. She was mostly under charter, sailing for New York-based Caribbean Cruise Lines on two–fourteen day itineraries. However, after that company went bankrupt in 1964 and the ship was sold to Norwegian buyers, who began using her as the *Viking Princess*. She sailed from many US east coast ports, including Boston, New York, Philadelphia, Port Everglades and Miami.

In otherwise bright Caribbean sunshine, the tragic fire aboard the cruise ship *Viking Princess* smolders in a view dated 8 April 1966. (ALF Collection)

The charred, blistered remains of the 537-foot long *Viking Princess*. (Fred Rodriguez Collection)

Hanseatic

Trouble before sailing from New York for Europe. While fire is often damaging, it is sometimes the smell of smoke that has doomed a passenger ship, especially an older one. Quite simply, the smell cannot be removed. 'The smell of smoke permeated the wood panels on older liners and, no matter how much cleaning and cleansing, it cannot be eliminated,' according to Captain James McNamara. 'The *Hanseatic* was a great loss because she was a great ship. Myself, I remember her as the *Empress of Scotland*, with her three checkered funnels, and then, in great contrast, as the rebuilt, modernized *Hanseatic*. It was one of the great conversions of the 1950s.'

Built as the *Empress of Japan* for Canadian Pacific's Vancouver–Far East service, she was renamed *Empress of Scotland* in 1942. She returned to commercial service, after war duties as a troopship, but on the company's Atlantic run between Liverpool and Montreal (with Caribbean cruising in winter from New York). A three-stacker, she was bought by the newly created Hamburg-Atlantic Line in 1957, totally rebuilt with two funnels and then recommissioned as the modernized, 1,252-passenger *Hanseatic* in the summer of 1958. She caught fire just hours before sailing to Europe, destined for Cherbourg, Southampton and Cuxhaven. On 7 Septemner 1966, while still berthed at New York's Pier 84, the liner caught fire. Due to depart that morning, the sailing was canceled, many passengers transferred to the nearby *Queen Mary* and the 672-foot-long *Hanseatic* was later taken to the Todd Shipyard in Brooklyn for inspection. It turned out, however, that repairs would be too costly given the 30,000-ton ship's thirty-six years of service. She was towed to Hamburg that fall and scrapped locally.

Smoke steams from the *Hanseatic* on the morning of 7 September 1966. (US Coast Guard)

New York fireboats stand watch over the *Hanseatic*. (ALF Collection)

Heraklion

Careless tragedy. The Bibby Lines' *Leicestershire* was built as a 76-passenger combination passenger-cargo liner for the UK–Burma run. She was, however, sold in 1964 to become the *Heraklion* for Greece's Typaldos Lines. She became quite a different ship, being rebuilt to carry up to 300 passengers, as well as trucks and cars. She actually ranked as the biggest ferry in the eastern Mediterranean at the time. Her new career was, however, was a short one. In stormy Aegean seas, on 7 December 1966, poorly secured cars and heavy trucks broke loose in the ship's garage spaces. The bow loading door was rammed, then broke open, and the 9,000-ton ship flooded quickly. Within hours, by the first daylight, the 498-foot-long ship was gone. Out of 268 passengers and crew, only 47 survived. Survivors were found clutching pieces of wood and debris, others clinging to the rocks of a nearby island. In a Greek government investigation that followed, the *Heraklion* was found to be unsafely loaded. The Typaldos Lines closed down, its fleet was seized and its owner sent to prison. Greek maritime safety standards were immediately upgraded.

Heraklion. (ALF Collection)

Bahama Star/La Janelle

Lashed by fierce winds! The *Bahama Star* was another aged cruise ship sailing between the Florida and the Bahamas in the 1960s. The 7,114-ton ship dated from 1931, having been the *Borinquen*, then the *Puerto Rico* and *Arosa Star*. She became the 735-berth *Bahama Star* in 1959, operated by Miami-based Eastern Steamship Lines. Finally retired in 1968, she might have gone to the scrappers, but found one last reprieve – as the *La Janelle*, intended to be a floating hotel/motel along the coast of southern California. Once there, at Port Hueneme, she was barely settled when fierce winds blew her ashore. She capsized and was later abandoned before being broken-up.

In happy times, the 1931-built *Arosa Star* would become a pioneer Florida cruise ship, the *Bahama Star*, in 1959. (Author's Collection)

Lashed by fierce waves off the southern California coast, the *Bahama Star*, by then renamed *La Janelle*, is driven ashore and wrecked. (US Coast Guard)

The little liner capsized once it hit the rocks at Port Hueneme. (Fred Rodriguez Collection)

Fulvia

Fire on a summer cruise. Built as the post-war flagship of the Norwegian America Line, the 16,844-grt *Oslofjord* was commissioned in the fall of 1949 for Atlantic crossings between Oslo, Copenhagen and New York. When that trade began to fall away in the mid-60s, however, she was chartered to the Greek Line and, beginning in 1969, to the Costa Line for fulltime cruising. Costa even renamed her as the *Fulvia*, and used her in alternating Mediterranean and Caribbean cruise service. It was during a summer cruise, on 19 July 1970, that she met her end. An engine room fire spread quickly, engulfed the 577-foot-long ship and left her a blistered wreck. She sank thirty-six hours later.

Norway's 577-foot-long *Oslofjord*, commissioned in 1949, later became the Costa Line cruise ship *Fulvia*. (ALF Collection)

Antilles

A sad end in the Caribbean. An engine-room fire started just before dinner, on 8 January 1971, aboard the French Line's 19,828-ton *Antilles*. Used on the Le Havre–West Indies route, the 778-passenger ship had to be abandoned, and was left eventually to lay on the rocks at Mustique and break in three pieces. Her 635 passengers and crew were rescued by the nearby *Queen Elizabeth* 2 and, coincidentally, by two French Line freighters.

The handsome *Antilles*. (Anton Logvinenko)

Queen Elizabeth/Seawise University

Death in Hong Kong. For thirty-two years, the 83,673-ton *Queen Elizabeth* ranked as the largest liner afloat. With the *Queen Mary*, she was part of that legendary pair of ocean liners, the Cunard 'Queens', as they were called. They were heroic troopships during the Second World War and hugely successful Atlantic express super liners. They ran near-continuous five-day crossings between New York and Southampton, with a stop at Cherbourg in each direction. But, in the rising age of the passenger jet, the *Queen Mary* was withdrawn in September 1967 and the *Queen Elizabeth* in October 1968. Even after her demise, the *Queen Elizabeth*'s size record remained until it was eclipsed by the 101,000-ton cruise ship *Carnival Destiny* in 1996.

The *Queen Mary* found further life as a hotel and museum at Long Beach, near Los Angeles, and the *Queen Elizabeth* was intended to have a similar role, but at Fort Lauderdale. The latter project failed entirely and in 1970 the 1,031-foot-long ship was auctioned off (for $6,000,000) for conversion into a cruise ship/floating university. Renamed *Seawise University*, she was to make worldwide voyages, which included a return to New York in the fall of 1972. But on 9 January 1972, while anchored in Hong Kong harbor on the eve of her departure for final dry docking in Japan, the former Cunard flagship caught fire. The blaze spread quickly. Some 900 workers and their families, onboard for a farewell party, escaped with only twenty-eight reported injuries. Later, reports suggested that the fire was a form of sabotage in the ongoing struggle between the communist Chinese and the Taiwanese.

As the fire smoldered on 10 January, the former *Queen Elizabeth* capsized, resting grotesquely at a 65 degree angle. The Japanese were soon called in and scrapped the wreck in two years. Today, her underwater remains are covered by an ultramodern container terminal.

Capsized and lying on her starboard side, the *Seawise University* – the former *Queen Elizabeth* – is beyond economic repair. (Des Kirkpatrick)

Once the largest liner afloat, the former *Queen Elizabeth* is no longer ready for passengers, but instead salvage crews and then Japanese scrappers. (Des Kirkpatrick Collection)

The wrecked *Seawise University* as seen from the stern. (Des Kirkpatrick Collection)

Meteor

Memory lane! Captain Helge Brudvik's very first passenger ship was the little *Meteor* of Norway's Bergen Line. Built in 1955, the 2,900-ton *Meteor* carried only 150 passengers in cabins (a third of the total) with private bathrooms; the others were without. There was an observation lounge with bar, a smoking room (as they called such rooms then), a small library and a lower-deck dining room. When in warm weather, there was no pool but two saltwater showers on deck instead. A handsome-looking, white-hulled ship, she cruised from Bergen in summer – on two-week itineraries, mostly – along the scenic Norwegian coast and occasionally up to remote Spitzbergen. In spring and fall, she was based at Monte Carlo, making two- and three-week Mediterranean cruises. In winter, she crossed over to San Juan, Puerto Rico and from there she made port-intensive trips to the lower Caribbean. In later years, in the late '60s, she spent her summers based at Vancouver doing weekly itineraries up to Alaska. She caught fire there in 1971, burned out and was said to be beyond repair. The Greeks swung in, however, bought the scorched ship, towed it to Greece and had it thoroughly rebuilt as the cruise ship *Neptune*. Run by the now defunct Epirotiki Lines, she did the Greek isles in summer; back to the Caribbean in winter.

The handsome *Meteor*. (Roger Scozzafava Collection)

Caribia

Pacific demise. Commissioned in late 1948, Cunard's 34,183-grt *Caronia* was quickly appraised as one of the most luxurious liners afloat. Although built to carry as many as 932 passengers, she mostly did long, expensive cruises and carried only up to 600 guests and often as few as 300. She had been called a 'floating country club.' Passengers came year after year, while a select few actually lived onboard, including one lady for fourteen years. The *Caronia* defined luxury cruising, but by the mid-1960s it began to lose passengers, grew aged and tired, and was part of that period's large-scale downsizing from Cunard. The 715-foot-long liner was sold, in 1968, to Greek interests, who planned to sail her on less-expensive Caribbean cruises from New York as the *Caribia*, beginning in the winter of 1969. On her second cruise, she had an engine room explosion, her passengers were sent home by air and the ship itself had to be towed to New York from the Caribbean. Thereafter, she languished around that port – often changing anchorages and piers. Finally, there was no hope of repairs or revival and the ship was auctioned off to Taiwanese scrap merchants. The *Caribia* departed from New York under tow on 27 April 1974. There were problems during the long, slow tow, and the worn, rust-stained liner met her end out in the Pacific. During a fierce storm, tug and ship sought shelter on Guam, but instead, on 13 August, the liner was blown onto a rocky breakwater and broke in three pieces. Her remains, soon declared a menace by local authorities, were promptly cut up.

The *Caribia*, formerly Cunard's luxurious *Caronia*, laid-up and moored between New York piers 84 and 86 in 1971. (Author's Collection)

The idle and bankrupt *Caribia* was later moored at Pier 56, which was ironically a former Cunard terminal, at the foot of West 14th Street in Manhattan. (Author's Collection)

Angelina Lauro

Galley fire: Happy cruise passengers were ashore on St Thomas in the Caribbean on 30 March 1979, only to return to their ship and find it engulfed in flames. That afternoon, a galley fire spread quickly aboard the 24,377-ton *Angelina Lauro*, owned by Italy's Flotta Lauro but chartered at the time to another Italian company, Costa Line. Built in 1939 as the Dutch East Indies flagship *Oranje*, the 656-foot ship remained in Dutch hands until 1964 when she joined Lauro and was completely rebuilt and modernized. At St Thomas, following the fire, the ship listed heavily to port; it was later righted, but found to be beyond economic repair. She was later sold to Taiwanese scrappers and would be towed to Kaohsiung for the final rites. There was more trouble, however. On 24 September, while empty and at the end of a towline, it sank.

The *Angelina Lauro* burning at its berth on St Thomas in the US Virgin Islands. (Author's Collection)

Leonardo da Vinci

'The *Leonardo da Vinci* was a fantastic ship! She was the Queen Bee of Italian shipping,' noted Steven Winograd, a superb passenger ship enthusiast and collector. 'She was every bit the embodiment of her nation, her name alone carried huge status. She had a "big ship" personality.'

Fred Rodriguez remembered the 33,340-ton *Leonardo da Vinci* as well. 'She was a beautiful ship with very gracious lines. I remember that up near the pilothouse there was a big, brass Catholic mural. It was a sort of shrine that looked like the traditional builder's plate. All the Italian Line passenger ships seemed to have these and they were supposed to be a good luck touch.'

The splendid, 761-foot-long *Leonardo da Vinci* ran the last of the celebrated Italian Line's transatlantic crossings when she sailed from New York to Genoa in June 1976. After a short stint doing Florida cruises, she was laid up at La Spezia in September 1978, sadly to never sail again. Rumors that she would be sold and possibly sail once more came to nothing. On 3 July 1980, a fire broke out in the ship's chapel and quickly spread. She was later towed outside the main harbor, burned herself out, then heeled over with a 60 degree list. She was raised in March 1981 and scrapped locally a year later.

The once-beautiful *Leonardo da Vinci* burning to death on 3 July 1980 at La Spezia, Italy. (Author's Collection)

The five pools (two were for children) are visible in this stern view of the 761-foot-long *Leonardo da Vinci*. (Antonio Scrimali)

Righted but scarred in rust and streaks of harbor mud, the *Leonardo da Vinci* was handed over to local scrappers at La Spezia in 1982. (Antonio Scrimali)

Prinsendam

Sunk off the coast of Alaska. An unusual ship within the Holland America fleet, the 8,566-ton, 374-passenger *Prinsendam* – commissioned in 1973 – was small by company standards. Purposely designed for Singapore- East Indies cruising, the ship later spent the summers up in Alaskan waters, cruising from Vancouver. During a positioning cruise from Vancouver to Singapore in October 1980, the 427-foot-long ship caught fire in the Gulf of Alaska. The ship was abandoned and all passengers and crew were saved. The ship drifted with hopes for salvage, but then sank several days later.

The smallish Holland America Line cruise ship *Prinsendam* drifts following a fire off the Alaskan coast in October 1980. (US Coast Guard)

71

Columbus C

Lost in a Spanish harbor. Commissioned in 1953, Swedish America Line's 21,141-ton *Kungsholm* was a very popular trans-Atlantic ship as well as cruise liner, but then changed hands, in 1965, to become North German Lloyd's *Europa*. In 1981, however, the 802-passenger ship was sold to Italy's Costa Line, becoming the *Columbus C*. Again, she was a popular cruise ship, but during a western Mediterranean cruise, on 29 July 1984, high winds blew the 600-foot-long liner against a breakwater at Cadiz, Spain. Afterward, the damaged ship attempted to reach her berth and offload her passengers, but then flooded and later capsized against the dock. She was later pumped out and then towed off to scrappers at Barcelona.

Flooded and resting on the harbor bottom, the *Columbus C* was beyond economic repair when this photo was taken in July 1984. Formerly the *Kungsholm* (1953), the stern of the *Sea Princess* can be seen on the left – another former *Kungsholm*, but dating from 1966. (Author's Collection)

Mikhail Lermontov and Admiral Nakhimov

Soviet passenger liners such as the 19,872-grt *Mikhail Lermontov* were often used for Western charters. During a cruise from Sydney, the 700-passenger ship sank hit a reef and sank in New Zealand waters on 16 February 1986.

A native of Odessa, Michael Tsaler recalled the many Soviet passenger ships that had Odessa as a homeport, many of which ran regular voyages along the Black Sea coast. Some were newer ships, such as the *Taras Schevchenko* and *Ivan Franko*, others were refitted, such as the *Leonid Sobinov* and *Feodor Shalyapin* (both ex-Cunarders). Others were quite old and of pre-Second World War vintage, usually former Nazi ships acquired as reparations or salvaged in the late 1940s, after the war ended.

One was the *Admiral Nakhimov*. She had been the *Berlin*, built in 1925 for the North German Lloyd and often used on the Atlantic run between Bremerhaven, Southampton, Cherbourg and New York. A rather ordinary ship, she had twin funnels but was rather small at a mere 15,000 tons. She did, however, carry as many as 1,300 passengers in three classes. Repainted in all-white and used as a Nazi hospital ship during the war years, she was a casualty in the end – or at least most onlookers thought so. She was sunk after striking a mine in the port of Swinemunde in February 1945, just three months before the Nazi surrender. Swinemunde later became part of East Germany and therefore Soviet-controlled territory. In a long, tedious process lasting four years, the badly damaged 572-foot-long liner was finally salvaged and then deemed worthy of full repairs. In an East German shipyard, these took almost eight years. She was finally recommissioned as the *Admiral Nakhimov* 1957. Among Soviet liners in the Black Sea, she was the queen of the fleet.

The *Nakhimov* sailed for an extraordinary sixty-one years, but then had a tragic demise. After colliding with another Soviet ship, the bulk carrier *Petr Vasev*, on the night of 31 August 1986, the old liner's days were over. The aged *Nakhimov* was mortally wounded and sank within minutes – with little time to fully abandon ship, it suffered the tragic loss of 398 passengers and crew. Even in the highly controlled Soviet Union, the news spread everywhere and was both horrifying and dramatic. The captains of both ships were later found to be drunk at the time of the collision, deemed guilty in the court hearings that followed and finally were sentenced to long prison terms. 'Many

people in Odessa were very angry. They lost family and friends,'
recalled Michael. He went on,

At the time, the *Nakhimov* was carrying far more passengers than
usual – family and friends of crew members who were sailing
free and so not on the manifest. It was a huge tragedy throughout
the USSR. It was the worst maritime tragedy in peacetime Soviet
history. I remember that, during the trial, the captains were kept in
the special KGB prison and were moved to the court room by way
of an underground tunnel and under heavy guard. Many people
wanted to kill them. They were kept in very tight steel cages when
they were moved about.

Two ex-German liners in Soviet hands – the *Rossia* (ex-*Patria*) is
to the left; the *Admiral Nakhimov* (ex-*Berlin*) is on the right. (ALF
Collection)

The 9,600-grt *Carnivale* might have been the first cruise ship in the Carnival Cruise Lines' fleet. Built in 1957, the 560-passenger liner had been the *Theodor Herzl* of Israel's Zim Lines. She was sold to AITS Travel, a forerunner to Carnival, but was never used. Later sold, she went to become the *Freeport I*, *Vera Cruz* and, by 1990, the *Sun Ambassador*. In 1991, however, while being refitted, she caught fire near Piraeus and later sank. She was later dismantled underwater and no fewer than seven pieces were salvaged and then scrapped. (Author's Collection)

A ship of great tragedy: The Long-idle Greek cruise sip *Athinai*, the former American liner *Santa Rosa*, built in 1932, had a reprieve in final years. She was used as a 'floating prop'. The 9,237-ton ship portrayed the *Titanic* in the 1978 film *Raise the Titanic*.

Oceanos

Moss Hill – a native of Zimbabwe – has long been an entertainer aboard cruise ships, but mostly those in African waters. Among a long list of ships, visiting varied ports, he has been involved in two ocean-liner tragedies – the sinking of the Greek *Oceanos* and the fatal fire aboard the infamous *Achille Lauro*. These days, Moss is cruise director of the elegant *Silver Whisper*.

Moss began aboard the 20,000-ton *Astor* of Cape Town-based Safmarine Lines, playing in a musical duo with his wife. 'My wife and I did some Cape Town–Southampton voyages and remember a huge storm that lasted for thirty-six hours on one of them,' he recalled. 'All the pool deck furniture was lost overboard. Afterward, we joined TFC Tours, a South African company, which chartered cruise ships such as the *Achille Lauro*. We did the Italy–Cape Town voyages and then the three or four months of summer [December through April] of South African cruises. I began to love ships more and more.'

TFC chartered the 15,000-ton *Oceanos* on a long-term basis in 1991. Owned by Epirotiki Lines, she had been the *Jean Laborde* of France's Messageries Maritimes, being built in 1952. She was rebuilt for Greek-flag cruising in the early '70s. Moss continues,

We joined the *Oceanos* in Cape Town for her cruises to Mauritius and also short trips between Cape Town, Port Elizabeth, East London and Durban. On one voyage, the ship's last, we were to sail at 5 p.m. in the evening, but were delayed due to fierce winds. It was even very windy on the quayside. We finally sailed, but the ship was tossing about. By dinner, I had to tie down the musical instruments in the lounge. Waiters were losing trays of food in the restaurant. Chairs were sliding about, moving away from the dining tables. After dinner, at about nine o'clock, it turned worse. Suddenly, the ship turned silent. We were powerless. Only the emergency lights were working. The guests began to worry. I started a sing-a-long, but the ship was lurching badly. We were broadside to the waves and so felt the greatest impact. The piano in the lounge got loose and crashed into the drums and the bulkhead. But, very strangely, there were no announcements or information from the bridge.

The 530-foot-long *Oceanos* was violently tossed about and began a severe list to starboard. Moss went on,

We were 8–10 miles off South Africa's Wild Coast between East London and Durban. Finally, we found the captain, who seemed almost stunned, smoking cigarette after cigarette and who finally ordered an 'abandon ship'. He said we would lower the lifeboats, but just as a precaution. We were not sinking nor were we afire. We could not even get a tug. He stressed that we were safe. There were no announcements nor any sounding of alarms, but only the loud rumbling of the waves lashing the ship. Suddenly, through a window, I saw a lifeboat being lowered. It was all a big mystery.

Everyone was now alarmed, very worried. I was just the guitarist but felt responsible, a great concern. I found the magician and together we decided to go below and check. The crew were yelling in five or six different languages and grabbing backpacks. Quickly, we realized there was danger! We asked: 'Are we really sinking?' We went down to D Deck and heard water, then saw water and realized we were sinking. We felt we had to help – to organize passenger evacuation. All the musicians helped and organized groups of twenty into the lifeboats. But it was difficult – they wanted to go to their cabins first and collect valuables. We collected life jackets and passed them to passengers. But still there were no announcements, no information, from the captain or the bridge.

The tension mounted.

We loaded lifeboats with passengers, but it was all very, very difficult. The ship was lurching badly to starboard. Within, chairs and tables and potted plants began sliding to starboard and crashing into the bulkhead. Outside, it was dark and very stormy. The setting could not have been worse. The lifeboats were swaying and mostly swinging outward. We desperately tried to keep the boats close to the side of the ship to board the very worried, very tense passengers. Some were terrified. We tried to load two or three lifeboats at one time, but they kept smashing into the side of the ship. The port side lifeboats were all but useless because of the severe list.

We knew we were in very real danger. After loading most of the boats, the magician and myself went up to bridge. But there was no one there. It was deserted. Charts and binoculars were scattered on the floor. The bridge was completely empty. By now, the starboard side was almost touching the water. The magician and I tried to call for help. We tried to figure out the black phone. We started saying 'May Day'.

One Asian ship, I think, couldn't understand and kept responding in their own language. They finally hung up on us. Finally, another ship, the *Nedlloyd Mauritius*, answered and its Dutch captain was very calm. He asked my rank. I said: guitar player. 'We will try to help you' was his strong, reassuring reply. But we did not know how to use the coordinator to relay our exact position. And we had only emergency lighting. Finally, we could see a ship off the bow, in the distant darkness of night. Three other ships were nearby at three o'clock in the morning. Most of the Greek officers had left in the lifeboats, but the captain was still missing. Later, we found him – with the radio officer – hiding in a corner and smoking cigarettes. They were in total denial. The captain seemed stunned but also ashamed. We realized he could not make a sound decision.

Most of the passengers were drifting in the fierce seas. They had been given flares and used them in the lifeboats. Back on the bridge and using that black phone, the magician and I finally reached the South African Air Force. They would send helicopters, but it would take three hours. By dawn, we were still waiting. We went below, to the restaurant, and found chairs, tablecloths and flowers floating. At that moment, we fully realized we were sinking quickly. We felt real and deep fear! The shop people and other musicians were still aboard, wearing lifejackets and gathered on the pool deck. They were struggling. They were sliding down the deck. The first light came at five o'clock and soon the first helicopter arrived. But there was further struggling. While the storm and the seas had abated, there was still a very strong wind. The rescue baskets from the helicopters swung like pendulums. The boutique manager was organizing this final evacuation – 228 were still aboard, half in the stern and half in the bow, out of 581 passengers and crew. We had to work fast – time was running out. One helicopter was over the bow, another over the stern. They were constantly lifting people off the ship. We all helped to attach harnesses to the anxious, scared passengers. The guests had to firmly hold onto railings or else slide downwards. My wife Tracy was the last woman onboard. The ship was lifting out of the sea, beginning to take her last plunge and going down by the bow. The stern section was rising higher and higher out of the water. The magician and I even tried to launch a Zodiac, but the outboard engine was quickly ripped off by the fierce seas.

In the end, only twelve people were left onboard. The magician remained on the bridge and continued radio contact. The ship was now lifting upward. We had to move faster than ever. The end was near. The water was now reaching us. Finally, my wife and I were harnessed, lifted by a helicopter and later brought ashore. We were safe. The passengers began cheering and singing for me. I smiled, but quickly collapsed with emotion on the beach.

The 10,970-grt *Oceanos*, owned by Greece's Epirotiki Lines, had been the French combination passenger-cargo liner *Jean La Borde* in her prior career. Vastly rebuilt for cruising, the 550-passenger ship was lost off the South African coast on 4 August 1991. (South African Air Force)

The *Oceanos* begins her end. (South African Air Force)

All of the port-side lifeboats aboard the 493-foot-long *Oceanos* are gone in this aerial view. (South African Air Force)

Sinking by the bow, the stern of the *Oceanos* lifts out of the water and begins its final plunge to the bottom. (South African Air Force)

Ocean Princess

Drama in the Amazon. The *Ocean Princess* was a popular cruise ship in the 1980s and her owners Ocean Cruise Lines were increasingly successful with some loyal followers. They also ran a second ship, the smaller *Ocean Islander*. The Fort Lauderdale-headquartered company was expanding – especially with new itineraries.

Cruises to South America, including around the Straits of Magellan and into the exotic Amazon River, were increasingly popular in the '80s and seen, at least by some cruising regulars, as appealing alternatives to the saturated, wintertime Caribbean. Ocean Cruise Lines wanted to tap into that market and so used their largest and best ship, the 12,000-ton, 470-passenger *Ocean Princess*. Historically, that sleek ship had been built in 1967 and owned by the Italians. She was first chartered to the then-new Princess Cruises and marketed as the *Princess Italia*. Costa bought her in 1973 and then sailed her as the *Italia* before Ocean Cruise Lines grabbed her in 1980. She then became the *Ocean Princess*, cruising the Caribbean in wintertime and then sailing on Mediterranean and North European itineraries for the remainder of the year. But her days were almost ended, however, when she nearly sank in Brazilian waters, in March 1993. Dr James Merrill was among her passengers at the time.

We were four and a half days into an Amazon River cruise, having just left Belem. As we left Belem harbor, we started to list and quite suddenly. It felt peculiar. The ship swung toward shore. It was all quite confusing. But then we learned the ship was taking on water in the theater on a lower deck. While we were told that there was no immediate danger, we were ordered to immediately go to our cabins, collect our lifejackets and proceed to the lifeboat stations. The ship was soon beached, stopped completely and quite still. No one was allowed below the Lido Deck and the watertight doors were closed. One woman was caught in the shower and others were in their swim suits. Certain cabins, the crew later announced, were safe and together we used flashlights to throw everything into suitcases. A local car ferry was brought alongside and the 300 passengers were sent to Belem, to the local Hilton Hotel. Another 60 of us, all in the American Express group, were sent to a smaller hotel.

Passengers had left hurriedly, leaving clothes, jewelry & medications behind. The ship's doctor was later supposed to help with medications, but never did. One entertainer lost all of his puppets. Another lost his guitar. Much later, there was some help. Passports were collected from the beached, half-sunk ship, and returned to each of us. Ocean Cruise Lines wanted to bring in a charter plane, a one-plane airline, to bring us to the United States, but the Brazilian government insisted that a Brazilian plane be used. Each of us was given a free ticket. When we finally left, the *Ocean Princess* was lying a few hundred yards from shore, aground, and was already being stripped by the locals.

The ship had hit river bed in the Amazon and began flooding. While she was later abandoned and declared a 'constructive loss,' the vessel was actually transferred to a salvage company for removal and then for local scrapping, but was in fact re-sold to Greek owners known as Ellis Marine. Scarred in rust and thick mud, she was carefully towed across the Atlantic to Piraeus in the summer of 1993, where I later saw her, laid-up and being further stripped of her passenger fittings. Small mountains of velore lounge and dining room chairs, for example, sat on the pierside on that sizzling August afternoon. A different area included stacks of stateroom mattresses. Another liner, the former Soviet *Alexandr Pushkin*, was at the adjacent dock, being rebuilt and refurbished as the *Marco Polo*. The former *Ocean Princess* was now renamed *Sea Prince I*. Later, she was sold to Louis Cruise Lines, a then-new cruise line interested in eastern Mediterranean itineraries, and renamed *Princesa Oceanica*. Still later, in 1996, she was placed on charter to Britain's Thomson Holidays and renamed *Sapphire*. Later used on charter to France Croisieres as well, she was later returned to Louis Cruise Lines' use and, in 2007, was sailing from Nice on cruises around the western Mediterranean. Unable to meet the new SOLAS safety standards of 2010, the forty-three-year-old *Sapphire* was retired, laid up and then sold to Indian scrappers two years later.

The burnt-out remains of another Epirotiki cruise ship, the *Pallas Athena*, which had been French Line's *Flandre* and later Costa's *Carla C*, as seen after a disastrous fire on 24 March 1994. Declared a loss, she was later towed to Turkey and demolished. (ALF Collection)

American Star

Left and abandoned. When it was launched and named on 31 August 1939 by Eleanor Roosevelt, wife of the American president, the 33,350-ton *America* would be the largest, fastest and probably most luxurious liner in the US merchant marine. Commissioned in the summer of 1940, the 723-foot-long liner later served as the troopship USS *West Point* before being restored as the 1,046-passenger *America* in 1946. Used in trans-Atlantic service until 1964, she was sold to Greek owners, becoming the *Australis, Italis, Noga, Alferdoss* and finally *American Star*. Idle in later years, she was to become a floating hotel at Bangkok when, as the *American Star*, she broke loose on 18 January 1994 during the long tow around Africa and out to the East. She drifted ashore in high winds, ran aground, was wrecked and later broke in two. The aft section later collapsed and fell into the sea and then, several years later, the fore section was gone as well.

Laid-up in a Greek backwater anchorage, the former *America/Australis/Italis* had fallen into deep decay. The liner was renamed *Alferdoss* by the time this photo was taken on 13 October 1992. (Peter Knego Collection)

Lashed by fierce Atlantic waves along the north side of the Canary Islands, the 723-foot-long hull of then renamed *American Star* broke in two. (Stephen L. Tacey Collection)

Only the forepart of the liner remains in this view. (Stephen L. Tacey Collection)

Still another view of the very sad ending of the former *America*. (Stephen L. Tacey)

By the end, the ship was covered in rust. (Stephen L. Tacey Collection)

The lower midsection is completely eroded in this view. (Stephen L. Tacey Collection)

The occasional photographer or even tourist would see the liner from the local seafront. (Author's Collection)

The entire remains would soon collapse into the sea. (ALF Collection)

Achille Lauro

Fiery flames off East Africa. Moss Hill, a native of Zimbabwe, first went to sea in 1985 – as a guitarist in the ship's band – aboard Safmarine Lines' *Astor*. With that 600-passenger ship, South Africa hoped to enter the luxury cruise trade and even revive the old mail service between South Africa and the UK. Moss himself quickly fell in love with the sea – and life aboard ships – and went on to work for nearly a dozen cruise lines over the next thirty years. He has served aboard the ships of Starlauro, MSC, Epirotiki, Dolphin Hellas, Holland America, Windstar, Princess and of course Safmarine. We met in the summer of 2014 when Moss was cruise director aboard Silversea's *Silver Whisper*. Moss is very friendly, talented and quite unique – he has survived the loss of two cruise ships: the sinking of the Greek liner *Oceanos* in 1991 and, three years later, the fiery demise of the *Achille Lauro*.

In those earlier years, Moss was a member of the band aboard the infamous *Achille Lauro* – present on what proved to be her very last voyage, no less. The 23,000-ton ship is perhaps best remembered, of course, for being hijacked by terrorists while on a Mediterranean cruise in October 1985. She soon became known throughout the world. Originally commissioned in 1947 as a Dutch liner, the *Willem Ruys*, she was thoroughly rebuilt and modernized in 1965/6 after being bought by Italian owners called Flotta Lauro. She was named for the owner, who had also been the longtime mayor of Naples. Together with the *Angelina Lauro*, the 1,500-passenger *Achille Lauro* was used in Europe–Australia and around-the-world liner services, and later for fulltime cruising. In her later years, she sailed on Mediterranean cruises in summer and, under charter to TFC Tours, on winter itineraries from South Africa. It was on one of these charter sailings that the 631-foot ship met her end.

Moss recalls,

We were on the 'positioning voyage' from Genoa to Durban via the Suez Canal. It was late November 1994, we had left Suez and were bound for a stop in Seychelles. The voyage had reached the halfway mark. It was a formal night, close to midnight. I was playing with the band when some passengers arrived. They'd come down from the top deck and told us that smoke was pouring not from the top but the bottom of the funnel. Dressed in my tuxedo, I stopped playing and rushed up to the top pool deck. Smoke was indeed pouring out of the funnel. I immediately sensed that there was a fire. Crew members arrived and we soon notified the bridge. Together, we began to undo the fire hoses.

The bridge soon told us that there was a fire down below, in the engine room. The captain finally came over the ship's public address system and told everyone that there was a fire onboard. We were ordered to get the passengers out of the public rooms and cabins, and on to the decks. Smoke was now pervading inside the ship, almost everywhere. It was now 1.30 a.m. and I was on the aft pool deck. We took pool towels, soaked them in pool water and used them to cover our faces. The captain soon reported, 'We are fighting fire – but it has been extinguished.'

Tragically, however, the intense heat in the engine room caused the fire to re-ignite. By 5.00 a.m., there was a call to abandon ship. We had 981 passengers and crew onboard. We had to organize evacuation and begin loading and then lowering the lifeboats, it all went very well at first – very organized and very calm. But then one passenger became terrified, had a heart attack and died very suddenly. His wife begged us to take his body into a lifeboat, but this had to be declined. He was never recovered. Another passenger, from Holland, wanted to return to his cabin to collect some valuable items. He returned to his cabin but was never seen again. Rather quickly, there was a third loss. A man said he needed his medication before going into a lifeboat or he would die quickly. I volunteered, went to his cabin, but the smoke was so thick I could not breathe. A fire door slammed and closed behind me. I was trapped. A sense of panic set in quickly. I was choking and soon unable to breathe because of the smoke. Fortunately, I found a small crew door – and climbed up quickly to the open deck. That man later died while in a lifeboat, and all because he was without his meds.

Moss himself was finally ready to board a lifeboat.

I was boarding one of the last two lifeboats. By now, the fire was spreading everywhere and smoke and flames were bursting through the lower deck portholes. We boarded the boats and then began to lower them, but it was to no avail. Quickly, we realized we could not lower those last two boats, being too difficult and dangerous to pass the roaring flames below that were reaching out from portholes and windows. We returned to the ship. We could see fire everywhere. But now what to do? Soon, one hundred of us, passengers and crew mixed together, went aft to the rope and chain deck. We decided to use the inflatable rafts. These inflatables were actually very heavy and difficult to toss over the rails and down to the sea. We also found a rope ladder, which was most likely used for pilots, and threw it over

the side as well. Crew members helped as passengers climbed down
the ladder to the rafts. Onboard, the fire was spreading quickly. The
disco on the aft deck was now burning and making thick smoke. We
put more pool towels around our heads as we launched and loaded
the inflatables. We launched the first, then the second and finally
the third. Unseen by us, however, a lifeboat filled with passengers
was trapped below, under the stern. Myself, I pushed the third
inflatable over the rail and, not seeing that lifeboat below because
of the thickening smoke, it landed on the lifeboat and immediately
killed one of the passengers. I was horrified – I killed a man! That
man thought he was being rescued, but then died in a dreadful
accident. I felt shock and horror – but tried desperately to keep some
composure. We had to lower the fourth and possibly the fifth and
sixth rafts. There was lots of elderly passengers and, using the rope
ladder, it was very difficult. One lady froze on the rope ladder and
then let go and fell into the water below. She was floundering about.
She would have drowned. I quickly grabbed a life jacket and jumped
into the sea. Landing in the water was fierce – it could break your
neck, even decapitate you. But I rescued her and got her into a raft.

Moss returned to the fiercely burning *Achille Lauro*.

We continued with evacuation – with the help of the twenty or so
very sturdy Israeli security agents we always carried on the *Achille
Lauro* [since the hijacking]. The fire was completely out of control
by now and the smoke was thicker than ever. The passengers in the
lifeboats below were beginning to panic. It was now very difficult
to get them into the rafts. I finally joined them, one of the last to
leave the doomed ship. I was exhausted and barely had the strength
to pull myself into the small opening of the tent-like raft. Floating
in the dark waters for six hours, we finally tied the five or six rafts
together as a group. We drifted away from the burning *Achille Lauro*,
which itself later seemed to drift in the opposite direction, over the
horizon and then to disappear. We began to sing a song called
'Le Nave Bleu' (the Blue Lady, the ship's nickname). In the final
sighting, she was burning from end to end – like a glowing inferno.
Almost everyone in the rafts was seasick and often very seasick.
We had bright sunshine by morning and slight swells before being
rescued by a cement freighter. We were taken to Djibouti.

Myself, I'd lost everything. However, TFC Tours almost
immediately chartered a replacement ship, called me and I was
back to sea in one week!

The former Dutch liner *Willem Ruys* has begun her conversion into the more contemporary in this view from 1964. (Author's Collection)

During her long refit, the *Achille Lauro* caught fire in August 1965 and was nearly destroyed. (Author's Collection)

The *Achille Lauro* burning off East Africa on 30 November 1994. (Author's Collection)

A photo taken at a Portland, Oregon, shipyard in October 1996. The liner *Constitution* would sink a little over a year later, on 17 November 1997, while under tow and en route to Far Eastern scrappers. (Hans Hoffmann)

Holland America's *Ryndam*, built in 1951, later became the Epirotiki Lines' flagship *Atlas*. Greatly modernized, she spent her final days as a casino ship, renamed as the *Pride of Mississippi*, *Pride of Galveston* and finally *Copa Casino*, along the US Gulf Coast before sinking in the Caribbean in March 2003. (Michael Cassar)

Sea Breeze I

Sinking off Virginia. Within ten years of its first passenger sailings aboard rebuilt ships, including austere, migrant-carrying ex-freighters, Italy's Costa Line introduced not only their first brand new liner, but one of the finest – and some added handsome – Italian liners of the 1950s. Company directors turned to a local shipyard, Ansaldo at Genoa, who proudly displayed the designs they had used for the splendid *Andrea Doria* and *Cristoforo Colombo* just a few years before and also for the forthcoming *Leonardo da Vinci*, which would be ready by 1960. The new Costa flagship would be something of a distant cousin to these ships. She was launched on 31 March 1957 as the *Federico C*.

The new ship, at 20,400 tons and with a capacity for 1,279 passengers in three classes, was immediately acclaimed as one of the finest ships of her time. Just after her maiden voyage from Genoa – on her regular run to Cannes, Barcelona, Lisbon and then across to Rio de Janeiro, Santos, Montevideo and Buenos Aires – in March 1958, she was also said to be the finest Italian liner on the Latin American run. Completely air-conditioned as well as stabilized, her level of decor (even in third class) was appraised as 'stunning contemporary'. She even surpassed, according to some, Italian Line's larger *Augustus* and *Giulio Cesare* on that same South Atlantic service. The accommodation aboard the 21-knot *Federico C* had at least five public rooms for each class, pools and lido decks for each, and all first-class and many second-class cabins had private facilities. And, of course, she proudly upheld the high standards in the kitchens and level of service for which Costa had become known. The new ship had one blemish: stability problems. 'Like the subsequent *Leonardo da Vinci*, the 606-foot-long *Federico C* had to be specially fitted with concrete ballast,' according to Maurizio Eliseo, one of the foremost Italian maritime historians and authors.

In 1983, Costa – then restyled as Costa Cruises – decided to reorganize as well as modernize its fleet, which was then the largest apart from the Soviet passenger ship fleet. They also decided to trim their fleet and so, among other dispositions, they sold the twenty-five-year-old *Federico C* to Florida-based Premier Cruise Lines. Premier wanted a ship for twice-weekly, three- and four-day cruises from Port Canaveral to the Bahamas that could be directly linked to their busy tour business with nearby Disney World. In fact, through a marketing arrangement, Premier Cruise Lines was soon also known as 'the Mickey Mouse cruise line.' Renamed *Royale*, the ex-Costa flagship was refitted, which included repainting the hull in bright red. She entered service in February 1984. In less than two years, success was at hand and she was joined by another Italian-built liner, Home Lines' brilliant, former *Oceanic*. Although not actually renamed, the two liners were advertised as the *Starship Royale* and *Starship Oceanic*. But once Premier bought another former Home Lines cruise ship, the *Atlantic*, the older, smaller *Royale* was back on the sales lists.

In February 1989, she hoisted the colors of Greek-owned Dolphin Cruise Lines (she was, in fact, registered to Panama-flag owners called Ulysses Cruses) and was renamed *Sea Breeze I* for seven-day Miami–Caribbean cruise service. She later made alternate cruises. The author was onboard in June 1999 when she sailed from Philadelphia on a two-night cruise 'to nowhere'. But most unusually, she poked into New York harbor on the first morning, sailed along the lower Hudson River, went north and passed under the George Washington Bridge, turned, reversed course and left the harbor just after lunch. 100 members of the Steamship Historical Society of America were aboard and I did the narrative, broadcast to the outer decks and public rooms, of New York harbor history, landmarks and notations.

Dolphin later fell into deep financial trouble and was acquired by Premier in 1997, so the *Sea Breeze I* returned to her previous owners. But then Premier itself collapsed in September 2000 and, to avoid being 'arrested' for debt, the *Sea Breeze I* all but dumped her final passengers at Halifax and was laid-up in that Nova Scotia port. But then, three months later, in December, while supposedly fleeing to foreign waters (to the Bahamas), she sank – reportedly under 'mysterious circumstances' – off the American East Coast. An alternate report was that she had in fact been bought by a holding company, Cruise Ventures, and was bound for a shipyard at Charleston, South Carolina. But in storm-tossed seas off the Virginia coast, her boilers allegedly broke, created a hole in the ship's side and she began to flood. Her small crew of thirty-four was rescued using helicopters by the US Coast Guard. Quietly, the former *Federico C* slipped under the waves. A subsequent investigation revealed that the forty-two-year-old liner was worth $5–6 million in scrap, but was insured for $20 million. Because the ship flew the Panamanian flag and was too far off the Virginia coast and therefore out of US legal domain, no full investigation of the sinking was ever carried out.

The *Independence* in happier days, berthed at Honolulu's Aloha Pier in July 2001. Just prior to being beached at Alang, India, in February 2010, the 683-foot-long ex-*Independence* (having by then been renamed *Oceanic* and then *Platinum II*) ran aground, broke in two, and had to be scrapped where she lay. (Author's Collection)

Well known from its starring role in the TV series *Love Boat*, the 646-passenger *Pacific Princess* is seen berthed at Lisbon. However, after being delivered to scrappers at Aliaga, Turkey, in August 2013, the former *Pacific Princess* partially capsized, prior to being demolished. (Luis Miguel Correia Collection)

Costa Concordia

Newsworthy and expensive. When the 114,147-grt *Costa Concordia* was commissioned in the summer of 2006, she and her subsequent Costa/Carnival sisters were among the largest liners built in Italy. The 3,780-passenger ship was on a Mediterranean cruise when, on 13 January 2012, the ship struck a rock in the Tyrrhenian Sea, on the western coast of Italy some sixty miles north of Rome. The grounding tore a 160-foot-long gash in the hull of the 952-foot liner, resulting in the flooding of her engine room, loss of power and the ship capsizing on her starboard side in shallow, coastal waters. It should have taken 30 minutes to evacuate the vessel, but in fact the abandon ship process took over six hours – 3,229 passengers and 1,032 crew were rescued while thirty-two perished. Among other problems, the captain had left the ship prematurely. The incident made international headlines for several days and all while the $600 million ship itself was written-off as uneconomic to repair.

The salvage, given to Dutch, Italian and American firms, took over two years and cost almost $800 million. The final costs, including repairs to the coastline, were later fixed at $2 billion, the most expensive salvage operation in history. In July 2014, the righted ship was towed – with a fourteen-ship escort – to nearby Genoa for scrapping. It would take another year before the remains of the *Costa Concordia* were then fully dismantled. Sadly, the largest liner listed in these pages had joined the list of passenger ship disasters.

The capsized *Costa Concordia* lies close to the Italian coast. (Author's Collection)

Partial demolition has begun for the *Costa Concordia* so as to increase refloating. (Author's Collection)

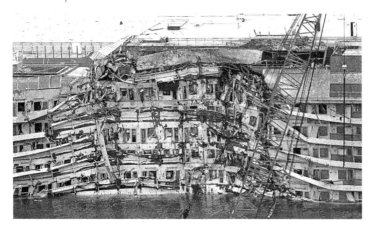

Once righted, the starboard side of the 951-foot-long *Costa Concordia* could be seen as badly damaged. (Author's Collection)

Further Reading

Braynard, Frank O. and Miller, William H., *Fifty Famous Liners, Vols 1–3*.

Braynard, Frank O. & Miller, William H., *Picture History of the Cunard Line 1840–1990*.

Kludas, Arnold, *Great Passenger Ships of the World Vol. IV*.

Kludas, Arnold, *Great Passenger Ships of the World, Vol. V*.

Mayes, William, *Cruise Ships* (5th edition).

Miller, William H., *Doomed Ships: Great Ocean Liner Disasters*.

Miller, William H., *Great American Passenger Ships*.

Miller, William H., *Great British Passenger Ships*.

Miller, William H., *Going Dutch: The Holland America Line Story*.

Miller, William H., *Picture History of British Ocean Liners: 1900 to the Present*.

Miller, William H., *Picture History of the Andrea Doria*.

Miller, William H., *Picture History of the French Line*.

Miller, William H., *Picture History of German and Dutch Passenger Ships*.

Miller, William H., *Picture History of the Italian Line*.

Miller, William H., *Pictorial Encyclopedia of Ocean Liners, 1860–1994*.

Miller, William H., *The Cruise Ships*.

Miller, William H., *Transatlantic Liners 1945–1980*.